T0312792

# WALKING LAKE COMO AND MAGGIORE

## DAY WALKS AND THE SENTIERO DEL VIANDANTE TREK IN THE ITALIAN LAKES

by Gillian Price

JUNIPER HOUSE, MURLEY MOSS,
OXENHOLME ROAD, KENDAL, CUMBRIA LA9 7RL
www.cicerone.co.uk

© Gillian Price 2023
Second edition 2023
ISBN: 978 1 78631 168 9
First edition 2019
Printed in Turkey by Pelikan Basim using responsibly sourced paper.
A catalogue record for this book is available from the British Library.
Maps by Nicola Regine.
All photographs are by the author unless otherwise stated.

*To dear Nicola, my special sherpa*

## Acknowledgements

First, a great big 'thank you' to Jonathan Williams of Cicerone for suggesting we explore these breathtaking lakes! We had no idea they were so beautiful.

I'd like to acknowledge helpful suggestions from Gillian Arthur and Mathilde Zuijdwegt of IAT Menaggio, as well as the enthusiastic Tourist Office staff of Bellagio, Cannero Riviera, Cannobio, Como, Gravedona, Lovere, Luino, Stresa and Verbania.

Big brother Marty made good use of his running shoes checking out alternate routes, and his taste buds in the quest for that perfect evening meal.

## Updates to this Guide

While every effort is made by our authors to ensure the accuracy of guidebooks as they go to print, changes can occur during the lifetime of an edition. Any updates that we know of for this guide will be on the Cicerone website (www.cicerone.co.uk/1168/updates), so please check before planning your trip. We also advise that you check information about such things as transport, accommodation and shops locally. Even rights of way can be altered over time. We are always grateful for information about any discrepancies between a guidebook and the facts on the ground, sent by email to updates@cicerone.co.uk or by post to Cicerone, Juniper House, Murley Moss, Oxenholme Road, Kendal LA9 7RL.

**Register your book:** To sign up to receive free updates, special offers and GPX files where available, create a Cicerone account and register your purchase via the 'My Account' tab at www.cicerone.co.uk.

*Front cover:* The path climbs away from Cannero Riviera (Walk 7)

# CONTENTS

Map key . . . . . . . . . . . . . . . . . . . . . . . . . . . . . . . . . . . . . . . . . . . . . . . . . . . . 5

INTRODUCTION . . . . . . . . . . . . . . . . . . . . . . . . . . . . . . . . . . . . . . . . . . . . 7
Plants and flowers . . . . . . . . . . . . . . . . . . . . . . . . . . . . . . . . . . . . . . . . . . . 9
Wildlife . . . . . . . . . . . . . . . . . . . . . . . . . . . . . . . . . . . . . . . . . . . . . . . . . . . . 10
Getting there . . . . . . . . . . . . . . . . . . . . . . . . . . . . . . . . . . . . . . . . . . . . . . . 10
Local transport . . . . . . . . . . . . . . . . . . . . . . . . . . . . . . . . . . . . . . . . . . . . . . 11
Information. . . . . . . . . . . . . . . . . . . . . . . . . . . . . . . . . . . . . . . . . . . . . . . . . 12
When to go . . . . . . . . . . . . . . . . . . . . . . . . . . . . . . . . . . . . . . . . . . . . . . . . 13
Accommodation. . . . . . . . . . . . . . . . . . . . . . . . . . . . . . . . . . . . . . . . . . . . . 14
Food and drink. . . . . . . . . . . . . . . . . . . . . . . . . . . . . . . . . . . . . . . . . . . . . . 15
What to take. . . . . . . . . . . . . . . . . . . . . . . . . . . . . . . . . . . . . . . . . . . . . . . . 17
Maps . . . . . . . . . . . . . . . . . . . . . . . . . . . . . . . . . . . . . . . . . . . . . . . . . . . . . 17
Dos and don'ts . . . . . . . . . . . . . . . . . . . . . . . . . . . . . . . . . . . . . . . . . . . . . . 17
Emergencies . . . . . . . . . . . . . . . . . . . . . . . . . . . . . . . . . . . . . . . . . . . . . . . . 18
Using this guide . . . . . . . . . . . . . . . . . . . . . . . . . . . . . . . . . . . . . . . . . . . . . 19

LAGO MAGGIORE. . . . . . . . . . . . . . . . . . . . . . . . . . . . . . . . . . . . . . . . . . 21
Walk 1    Stresa to Belgirate . . . . . . . . . . . . . . . . . . . . . . . . . . . . . . . . . . 29
Walk 2    From the Mottarone to Baveno . . . . . . . . . . . . . . . . . . . . . . . . 33
Walk 3    Monte Orfano and Lago di Mergozzo . . . . . . . . . . . . . . . . . . . 38
Walk 4    Cavandone on Monterosso . . . . . . . . . . . . . . . . . . . . . . . . . . . 43
Walk 5    Ghiffa Sanctuary Loop. . . . . . . . . . . . . . . . . . . . . . . . . . . . . . . 47
Walk 6    Villages above Cannero. . . . . . . . . . . . . . . . . . . . . . . . . . . . . . 51
Walk 7    The Cannero–Cannobio Traverse . . . . . . . . . . . . . . . . . . . . . . . 55
Walk 8    Monte Carza . . . . . . . . . . . . . . . . . . . . . . . . . . . . . . . . . . . . . . 59
Walk 9    Val Cannobina . . . . . . . . . . . . . . . . . . . . . . . . . . . . . . . . . . . . 63
Walk 10   Cannobio–San Bartolomeo in Montibus Circuit. . . . . . . . . . . . 69
Walk 11   Monteviasco . . . . . . . . . . . . . . . . . . . . . . . . . . . . . . . . . . . . . . 73
Walk 12   Sasso del Ferro . . . . . . . . . . . . . . . . . . . . . . . . . . . . . . . . . . . . 78

LAGO DI COMO. . . . . . . . . . . . . . . . . . . . . . . . . . . . . . . . . . . . . . . . . . . 81
Walk 13   Moltrasio to Laglio . . . . . . . . . . . . . . . . . . . . . . . . . . . . . . . . . 90
Walk 14   Pigra to Colonno. . . . . . . . . . . . . . . . . . . . . . . . . . . . . . . . . . . 93
Walk 15   Colonno to Cadenabbia on the Greenway. . . . . . . . . . . . . . . . 96
Walk 16   San Martino Circuit. . . . . . . . . . . . . . . . . . . . . . . . . . . . . . . . . 101

Walk 17   The Bocchetta di Nava Traverse........................... 104
Walk 18   Crocetta ............................................. 108
Walk 19   Val Sanagra.......................................... 111
Walk 20   Rifugio Menaggio and Monte Grona...................... 116
Walk 21   San Domenico and the Santuario di Breglia ............... 121
Walk 22   Gravedona to Domaso ................................. 123
Walk 23   Domaso to Gera Lario................................. 127
Walk 24   Around Bellagio ...................................... 133
Walk 25   Belvedere del Monte Nuvolone......................... 137
Walk 26   Monte San Primo ..................................... 141
Walk 27   The Strada Regia from Pognana Lario to Torno.............. 145
Walk 28   Brunate to Torno Path ................................ 150

**SENTIERO DEL VIANDANTE TREK**............................... 156

**Appendix A**   Route summary table ............................. 182
**Appendix B**   Glossary of Italian–English terms .................... 184

## Mountain safety

Every mountain walk has its dangers, and those described in this guidebook are no exception. All who walk or climb in the mountains should recognise this and take responsibility for themselves and their companions along the way. The author and publisher have made every effort to ensure that the information contained in this guide was correct when it went to press, but, except for any liability that cannot be excluded by law, they cannot accept responsibility for any loss, injury or inconvenience sustained by any person using this book.

To call out the Mountain Rescue, ring 118: this will connect you via any available network. Once connected to the operator, ask for *Soccorso Alpino*.

# Map key

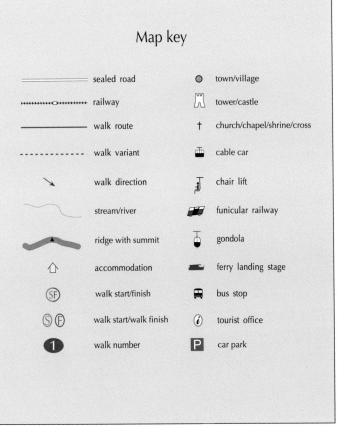

| | | | |
|---|---|---|---|
| ══════════ | sealed road | ◉ | town/village |
| ┈┈┈○┈┈ | railway | 🏰 | tower/castle |
| ────── | walk route | † | church/chapel/shrine/cross |
| ‑ ‑ ‑ ‑ ‑ | walk variant | | cable car |
| ↘ | walk direction | | chair lift |
| 〜 | stream/river | | funicular railway |
| | ridge with summit | | gondola |
| ⌂ | accommodation | | ferry landing stage |
| SF | walk start/finish | | bus stop |
| S F | walk start/walk finish | ⓘ | tourist office |
| 1 | walk number | P | car park |

Monte Zeda dominates the western branch of Val Cannobina, Lago Maggiore (Walk 9)

# INTRODUCTION

Nothing in the world could compare to the charms of
these days spent on the Milanese lakes.
*Stendhal (1783–1842)*

Beyond Bellano is the Dervio peninsula in upper
Lago di Como (Sentiero del Viandante trek)

A duo of magnificent lakes stands out in the north of Italy at the foot of the Alpine chain on the border with Switzerland. Their glittering expanses have been visited by English-speaking travellers since the days of the Grand Tour for their exquisite villas and lush gardens where camellias and rhododendrons spill over terraces.

Nowadays Lago Maggiore and Lago di Como are well-known destinations for holidaymakers from the four corners of the globe attracted by relaxing ferry cruises and romantic waterfront restaurants. Yet only steps beyond the popular lakesides, a wonderful world of old villages and verdant alpine landscapes waits to be discovered. The 28 walks and short trek described in this guidebook wander around these beautiful lakes, making use of a vast network of age-old paved mule tracks through woodland and pasture once used to link remote hamlets and alpine valleys in the interests of trade, pilgrimage and travel. Walking enthusiasts of all levels of experience and ability can enjoy well-marked routes ranging from leisurely lakeside promenades for novice walkers up to strenuous climbs up panoramic peaks. There is something for everyone. Twenty-eight of these walks can each be fitted into a single day, while another, a mini trek stretching over five days, can also be cut into one-day stages if desired. And what's more, all the walks can be accessed by the excellent system of local public transport, be that ferry, train, bus, cable car or chair lift.

The two lakes are strikingly beautiful yet surprisingly different in flavour and atmosphere. So how do you decide which one to start with? Laidback Maggiore boasts a bevy of picturesque islands-cum-villages backed by lofty mountains dotted with old hamlets. On the other hand, quintessentially romantic Como is pure elegance

in terms of its villas and gardens, although the lake's edges also feature surprisingly sheer cliffs and dramatically scenic pathways. Further enticing details can be found in the individual lake chapters. Further east lie Lago di Garda and Lago d'Iseo which are covered in the separate Cicerone guide *Walking Lake Garda and Iseo*. Rest assured that once your enthusiasm is fired you'll want to see them all!

The lakes owe their formation to the massive glaciers that slowly spread down from the Alps towards the Italian plains hundreds of thousands of years ago. The glaciers carried with them rock debris which was bulldozed into long uniform ridges known as moraines. When temperatures rose – around 12,000 years ago – the ice began to melt and retreat, leaving elongated troughs which filled with water, forming the

*The beautiful grounds of Villa Melzi, Lago di Como (Walk 26)*

## THE LINEA CADORNA

In the period preceding World War I, the fledgling Republic of Italy feared an invasion from Germany and Austria by way of neutral Switzerland, and set on the idea of protecting its frontiers. The Linea Cadorna, named after its principal creator General Luigi Cadorna, became reality between 1912 and 1916. An incredible 40,000 men were put to work constructing a man-made barrier stretching across the mountain tops and valleys of the alpine foothills up to the 2000m mark, from Passo del Sempione, northwest of Lago Maggiore all the way to Chiavenna well north of Lago di Como, and touching on the shores of the great lakes. A total of 296km of roads, 398km of mule tracks and 72km of trenches were constructed, as well as lookout posts, command structures and barracks (thankfully never put to the test), sehich are till in remarkably good condition. Sections of the Linea Cadorna are visited on Walks 3, 7 and 8 on Lago Maggiore, as well as Walk 18 on Lago di Como.

spectacular lakes. Lying on a north–south axis, they resemble deep fjords, wedged between line after breathtaking line of rugged mountain ridges rising well over 2000m. Rivers and streams running straight off the Alps feed the lakes, which take until midsummer for their crystal-clear waters to reach 24°C, a bearable temperature for swimming.

## PLANTS AND FLOWERS

The Italian lakes offer much for flower lovers to admire as the equable climate and a broad altitude range guarantee myriad Mediterranean as well as alpine species. Spontaneous blooms complement the magnificent exotic plants and trees found in the many formal villa gardens.

Exquisite wildflowers can be expected as early as April and May (spring) at lower altitudes, while the main display on the high alpine mountain ridges gets underway in June. High stone walls are often adorned with magnificent bouquets of straggling caper plants, their open white petals brandishing purple stamens. It is their buds, picked and pickled or salted, which are familiar ingredients of Italian cuisine. Blooms and colours continue through to late summer (August–September), while autumn (October) brings russet hues in woods and forests.

Other highlights include brilliant orange lilies in shady meadows, the concentrated blue-purple willow-leaved gentian that blooms in gay clumps on open grassland, and true alpine species such as cinquefoil and alpine cornflower. Enthusiasts will appreciate the Cicerone mini guide *Alpine Flowers*.

## WILDLIFE

One presence, albeit mysterious, that sets Lago di Como apart from the other northern Italian lakes is the 'dreaded' Lariosaurus, a mythical reptilian creature said to resemble the famed Loch Ness monster in appearance and behaviour. However, Larrie (as it has been nicknamed) is reputedly smaller – under 2m in length – but much more ferocious than its Scottish counterpart!

Walkers in woods will often notice hoof marks in the mud and scratchings and diggings in the undergrowth, a sure sign of the presence of wild boar. Actual sightings are extremely rare as the creatures are very timid.

Chances are better of spotting roe deer flitting between trees, while higher rocky terrain is home to the dainty goat-like chamois, recognisable for their trademark crochet-hook horns and dark-patched rear quarters. Grassland over the 800m mark is

*A marmot at its burrow*

home to colonies of endearing alpine marmots, often seen dashing across the meadows on a quest for sugary wildflowers to feast on.

The area is also home to a superb range of birds of prey, such as kites and eagles, soaring overhead looking out for a meal, while myriad timid songbirds provide sonorous entertainment from the safety of tree cover.

## GETTING THERE

Both lakes can be easily accessed by overseas visitors. Specific details for getting around locally are given in the introduction to each chapter.

**By air**
Milan's airports, Malpensa (www. milanomalpensa-airport.com) and Linate (www.milanolinate-airport. com), are handy for both Lago di Como and Lago Maggiore. Bergamo's Orio Al Serio airport (www.sacbo.it) can also be used for Lago di Como.

**By train**
A couple of international train lines between Switzerland and Italy come in handy. The Brig to Milano Centrale run via Domodossola calls in at Stresa on Lago Maggiore. For Lago di Como there are direct Zurich–Milano Centrale trains via Chiasso to San Giovanni station at Como. (Italian trains www.trenitalia.com, Swiss rail www.sbb.ch.)

## LOCAL TRANSPORT

The extensive network of trains, buses, ferries and cable cars around and across Lago Maggiore and Lago di Como is easy to use and unfailingly reliable. All the walks in this guidebook start and finish at a point that is accessible by local public transport (and the book was researched using it). Local bus drivers know the roads and conditions like the back of their hands, leaving passengers free to sit back and enjoy the views. So you never need to think of hiring a car or taking your own and so can avoid contributing to air pollution and traffic congestion in these magical places.

Generally speaking, bus schedules follow the Italian school year, with extra runs during term time. Slightly reduced summer timetables correspond to the main holidays, which fall mid-June through to mid-September. Full ferry services are timetabled from March/April through to October/November; during winter services are cut back drastically and some lines are suspended. Exact dates vary from year to year, company to company and region to region, but

## USEFUL EXPRESSIONS

**These expressions may come in useful when purchasing tickets.**

| | |
|---|---|
| One ticket/two tickets to Monteisola, please. | *Un biglietto/due biglietti per Monteisola, per favore.* |
| single | *andata/corsa semplice* |
| return | *andata e ritorno* |
| How much is that? | *Quanto costa?* |
| platform | *binario* |
| timetable | *orario* |
| Thank you | *Grazie* |
| You're welcome | *Prego* |

**The following words may be helpful for understanding timetables.**

| | |
|---|---|
| Change at.../connection | *Cambio a.../coincidenza* |
| summer/winter | *estivo/invernale* |
| working days (Monday to Saturday) | *feriale* |
| holidays (Sundays and public holidays) | *festivo* |
| daily | *giornaliero* |
| Monday to Friday/Saturday | *lunedì a venerdì/sabato* |
| shuttle service | *navetta* |
| strike | *sciopero* |
| during school term | *scolastico* |

can easily be checked on the websites listed under the individual lakes.

Reasonable pricing prevails: for instance, at the time of writing, the ferry from Intra to Laveno on Lago Maggiore cost €3.40. Over 65s are entitled to reductions (Monday–Friday). Day tickets are available – ask for *biglietto di libera circolazione*. A local train ticket from Belgirate to Stresa costs €2.10, while the funicular from Como to Brunate is €3.10 one way or €5.70 return. The cable cars tend to be more expensive, although the Argegno–Pigra run on Lago di Como is €3.50.

Bus tickets should usually be purchased before a journey, either at the bus station or newsstands or tobacconists displaying the appropriate logo for the relevant transport company. Should a railway station be unmanned and have no automatic machine (common at minor stations), ask the conductor on board the train to sell you a ticket. At the larger stations, remember to validate (stamp) train tickets at one of the machines on the platform before boarding, so as to avoid a fine.

Specific details for buses, trains, ferries, cable cars and taxis are given at the beginning of each chapter.

## INFORMATION

The Italian Tourist Board (www.enit.it) has offices all over the world and can help those planning to visit the Italian lakes with general information.

Information on accommodation, transport and what to see can be obtained from local tourist information offices and websites.

### Lago Maggiore

- Cannero Riviera
  tel 0323 788943
  www.cannero.it
- Cannobio tel 0323 71212
  www.procannobio.it
- Laveno tel 0332 667223
  www.stradasaporivallivaresine.it
- Luino tel 0332 543546
  www.comune.luino.va.it;
  www.vareselandoftourism.it
- Stresa tel 0323 31308
  www.stresaturismo.it;
  www.visitstresa.com
- Verbania: Pallanza
  tel 0323 503249
  www.verbania-turismo.it;
  Intra tel 348 2547482

*A gondola rises to dizzy heights over Laveno on Lago Maggiore (Walk 12)*

*Bellagio and far-off Monte Legnone from the belvedere, Lago di Como (Walk 27)*

## Lago di Como

- Bellagio tel 031 951555
  www.promobellagio.it
- Como tel 031 269712
  www.visitcomo.eu
- Domaso tel 324 0914635
  www.visitdomaso.com
- Gravedona tel 0344 85005
  www.visitgravedona.it
- Lecco tel 0341 481485
  www.eccolecco.it
- Menaggio tel 0344 32924
  www.menaggio.com

### WHEN TO GO

The lakes are renowned for their mild climate. Temperatures range from around 13°C in December to the high 20s in July.

Generally speaking, the months of spring through to early summer (March to June) are recommended for walking in the area as temperatures are usually reasonable, the vegetation is a brilliant green and the flowers blooming. However, September and October are wonderful as well, with marginally fewer visitors and clear, crisp conditions once any summer haze has dissipated. At low altitudes, midsummer (July and August) can get quite hot – up to 30°C – although an afternoon breeze is nearly always guaranteed. Of course, the heat can be tempered with a dip in a lake (or your hotel swimming pool) or better still, a walk at an alpine elevation.

The high-altitude walking routes are out of bounds throughout the winter months due to snowfall. However, crisp, sunny winter days can make for perfect low-altitude walking with brilliant visibility. Be aware that ferry

*Stage 2 of the Sentiero del Viandante sets out from Abbadia Lariana*

services are reduced from November through to March, and much accommodation closes, as do villas and gardens.

The lakes can get very busy on the main Italian public holidays: 1 January (New Year), 6 January (Epiphany), Easter Sunday and Monday, 25 April (Liberation Day), 1 May (Labour Day), 2 June (Republic Day), 15 August (Ferragosto), 1 November (All Saints), 8 December (Immaculate Conception) and 25–26 December (Christmas and Boxing Day).

## ACCOMMODATION

The lakes have a huge range of accommodation in hotels, B&Bs, hostels, self-catering apartments, campsites and even mountain huts. Suggestions in the middle price range are given in the introduction to each lake chapter, while for the Sentiero del Viandante trek, options are listed at the end of each stage. Naturally, a host of alternatives can be found on the web.

Book well in advance around the Italian public holidays (see above) and the peak months of May and September. Remember that much accommodation – but by no means all – closes over the winter, usually from November to March, so check beforehand if planning a visit in low season.

If you call from overseas, preface phone numbers with +39 (the country code for Italy). Always include the initial 0 of the area code – the exceptions are mobile phone numbers which begin with 3 and emergency numbers such as 118.

## FOOD AND DRINK

Special treats are in store for the taste buds of adventurous eaters. The walking areas featured in this guide belong to the northern Italian regions of Piemonte and Lombardia, each with unique traditional gastronomic specialities. Generally speaking, the best rule in a restaurant is to ask for the day's speciality, which will invariably feature seasonal locally sourced products. *Che cosa avete oggi?* means 'What's on today?' In terms of dinner, Lombardia spells risotto heaven and foodies will find plenty to get their forks into. Where available, go for the ultimate, *risotto alla milanese*, creamy rice cooked in a delicate meat broth, fragrant with saffron and often twinned with

*ossobuco*, tender braised veal shank. Pasta everywhere comes in a bewildering array of shapes and sauces. Unusual choices include *Piemontese panciotti*, pasta parcels stuffed with fish, or crescent-shaped vegetable and meat *agnolotti*.

In the Brescia district of Lombardia country restaurants do *spiedo* at the weekend: a selection of meats liberally seasoned with fresh herbs is gently spit-roasted and served with polenta (cornmeal). Traditionally, that once meant *uccellini*, birds hunted in the hills over the autumn months.

Freshwater fish from the lakes is a constant on menus. The most common is *coregone* – also known as *lavarello* – which translates as whitefish. Its pale flesh, delicate and soft, is

*The glorious waterfront at Bellagio on Lago di Como*

perfectly suited to a quick grilling or frying. Diners on Lago di Como may also be offered *missoltino* or *agone*, a type of small pilchard that has been salted and preserved (the English name is 'twaite shad'). Look out too for the curiously named fried bleak (*alborella*), a small silvery fish common in Lago Maggiore.

For picnic lunches, neighbourhood grocery shops or small supermarkets are usually happy to make up a fresh bread roll (*panino*) with your choice of filling. Any of the renowned Italian cured meats such as *prosciutto crudo* are perfect. Salami made with goat meat is a variant on the more usual pork. One unparalleled treat found in the mountains of Piemonte is *violino d'agnello*, lamb that has been softened with lard; sliced transparently thin, it melts in the mouth. Cheeses crafted from cow (*mucca*), sheep (*pecora*) or goat (*capra*) milk come in a huge range: soft, smooth, crumbly, tangy (and downright mouldy and stinky at times), as the mouth-watering display at any delicatessen can attest.

Wine lists offer a kaleidoscope of flavours and Piemonte boasts memorable reds such as Barbera, Nebbiolo and Dolcetto. Lombardia's Valtellina at the top of Lago di Como is also home to excellent red wine, the ilk of Inferno and Sassello.

A note on drinking water: Italian domestic tap water (*acqua da rubinetto*) is always safe (*potabile* means drinkable), and by law is meticulously tested on a regular basis. You

*Many grape varieties flourish on sunny slopes around the lakes*

can request it in any restaurant or café instead of bottled mineral water, which needs to be transported at a high cost to the environment. Fill up your drinking bottle at the village taps and fountains, still commonplace in most alpine villages and hamlets.

Breakfast in Italy tends to be a simple affair. Most Italians take a coffee as *cappuccino* (with frothy milk) or *espresso* (a strong black concentrated shot), usually accompanied by a croissant, while standing up at the local café. However luckily for visitors, these days most middle-range hotels and B&Bs do a decent buffet breakfast with fruit, cereals, eggs, bread and a choice of beverage.

All the major towns and villages have a grocery store (*alimentari*) or supermarket, not to mention an ATM.

## WHAT TO TAKE

- Sun protection: hat, high-factor cream and sunglasses
- Bottle for drinking water
- Small daypack: shoulder and hand-held bags are unwise, as it's safer to have hands and arms free while walking
- Lightweight trekking boots, or decent pair of trainers or sports shoes, with good grip and thickish soles to protect your feet from loose stones; sandals are quite unsuitable and can be dangerous
- Trekking poles for the high mountain routes
- Waterproof gear including lightweight jacket, rucksack cover and overtrousers
- T-shirts and shorts during spring/summer, layered with a light sweater or shirt for cooler conditions
- Autum/winter visitors should pack warm clothes: long trousers, fleece or pullover, hat and gloves
- Basic first-aid kit
- Whistle, headlamp or torch for calling for help in an emergency
- Maps (see below) and compass

## MAPS

Sketch maps are provided for each walk in this guidebook. In many cases these are sufficient, in combination with the walk description. However, it is always a good idea to get hold of larger maps of the area for a number of valid reasons: they put places in a wider context, help you identify other points of interest, plot your own routes, and last but not least, are an essential tool for orientation if you lose your way or decide to change route. A good range of walking maps is available for the lakes, and specific information is given in the introduction to each chapter. Some maps are available overseas at outdoor stores and bookshops, several can be downloaded from websites, while others are sold locally at the lakes.

## DOS AND DON'TS

- Don't set out late in the day, even on a short walk. Always allow extra time for detours and wrong turns.
- Do find time to get in decent shape before setting out on your holiday, as it will maximise enjoyment. The wonderful scenery will be better appreciated when you're not in a state of exhaustion, and healthy walkers react better in an emergency.
- Don't walk on your own. Stick with your companions and don't lose sight of them; remember that the progress of the group should match that of the slowest member.

- Don't be overly ambitious; choose routes suited to your ability (and to that of the group). Read the walk description carefully before setting out.
- Avoid walking in brand new footwear, to reduce the likelihood of blisters; leave those old worn-out shoes at home, as they may be unsafe on slippery terrain. Choose your footwear carefully; comfort is essential.
- Check the weather forecast locally if possible and don't start out, even on a short route, if storms are forecast: paths can get slippery and mountainsides are prone to rockfalls
- Carry weatherproof gear at all times, along with food and plenty of drinking water
- In electrical storms, don't shelter under trees or rock overhangs, and keep away from metallic fixtures
- **Do not** rely on your mobile phone in an emergency as there is often no signal in the mountainous areas
- Carry any rubbish back to the village, where it should be disposed of correctly. Even organic waste such as apple cores and orange peel is best not left lying around as it is an eyesore for other visitors and upsets the diet of animals and birds.
- Be considerate when making a toilet stop. Carry a supply of small plastic 'doggy' bags to deal with paper and tissues.
- Finally, don't leave your common sense at home

## EMERGENCIES

For medical matters, walkers who live in the EU need a European Health Insurance Card (EHIC), while UK residents require a UK Global Health Insurance Card (GHIC). Holders of both are entitled to free or subsidised emergency treatment in Italy, which has an excellent public health system. Australia has a reciprocal agreement – see www.medicareaustralia.gov.au. Those from other countries should make sure they have appropriate coverage.

Travel insurance for a walking holiday is also strongly recommended, as the costs of rescue and repatriation can be considerable. Membership of the Italian Alpine Club CAI www.cai.it is open to everyone and includes insurance for mountain rescue operations all over Europe.

The following services may be of help should problems arise:
- General emergency tel 112
- *Polizia* (police) tel 113
- Health-related emergencies including ambulance (*ambulanza*) and mountain rescue (*soccorso alpino*) tel 118
- 'Help!' in Italian is *Aiuto!*, pronounced 'eye-you-tow'. *Pericolo* is 'danger'.

*Beautiful lake views from the San Martino route (Walk 16)*

Should help be needed during a walk, use the following internationally recognised rescue signals: **six** signals per minute, either visual (waving a handkerchief or flashing a torch) or audible (shouting or whistling), repeated after a pause of one minute. The answer is **three** visual or audible signals per minute, to be repeated after a one-minute pause. Anyone who sees or hears a call for assistance must contact the nearest source of help, – a mountain hut or police station for example – as quickly as possible.

These hand signals (below) could be useful for communicating at a distance or with a helicopter.

## USING THIS GUIDE

This guidebook contains a selection of the multitude of walking routes on

**Help required**
Raise both arms above head to form a 'Y'

**Help not required**
Raise one arm above head and extend the other downward, to form the diagonal of an 'N'

Lago Maggiore and Lago di Como in northern Italy. (A second Cicerone guidebook covers *Walking Lake Garda and Iseo*.) Visitors wishing to do more – and there are plenty more! – can enquire at the local Tourist Offices and even join a guided walk if desired.

Many routes are waymarked with official CAI (Italian Alpine Club) red/white paint stripes together with an identifying number, to be found along the way on prominent stones, trees, walls and rock faces.

Each walk description is preceded by an information box containing the following essential data:

- **Start**
- **Finish**
- **Distance** in kilometres and miles
- **Ascent/Descent** Height gain and loss are an indication of effort required and need to be taken into account alongside difficulty and distance when planning the day. Generally speaking, a walker of average fitness will cover 300m (about 1000ft) of ascent in one hour.
- **Difficulty** Each walk has been classified by grade, although adverse weather conditions will make any route more arduous.
  - Grade 1 Easy route on clear tracks and paths, suitable for beginners.
  - Grade 2 Paths across hill and mountain terrain, with lots of ups and downs; a reasonable level of fitness is required
  - Grade 3 Strenuous, entailing some exposed stretches and possibly prolonged ascent. Experience and extra care are recommended.
- **Walking time** This does not include pauses for picnics, views, photos or nature stops, so always add on a good couple of hours when planning your day. Times given during the descriptions are intermediary (as opposed to cumulative).
- **Access** Information on how to get to the start point and away from the finish.

Within the walk descriptions, 'path' is used to mean a narrow pedestrian-only way, 'lane' is unsurfaced but vehicle width, and 'road' is surfaced and open to traffic unless otherwise specified. Compass bearings are in abbreviated form (N, S, NNW and so on), as are right (R) and left (L). Reference landmarks and places encountered en route and shown on the accompanying map are in bold type, with altitude in metres above sea level given as 'm', not to be confused with minutes (abbreviated as min). Note that 100m = 328ft.

# LAGO MAGGIORE

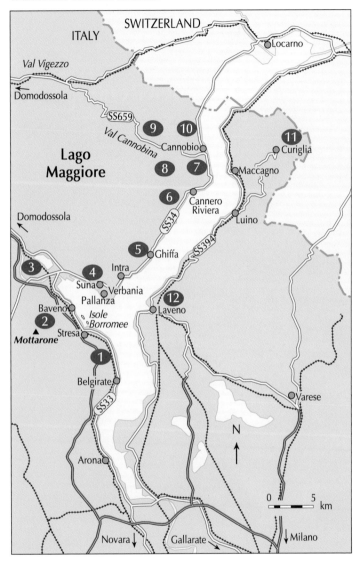

# INTRODUCTION

*It is the most voluptuous place I have ever seen in the world.*
*Nature enchants you with a thousand unknown fascinations and*
*you feel in a state of rare sensuality and refinement.*
*Gustave Flaubert, 1845*

Picturesque Lago Maggiore has been working its magic on writers and visitors for centuries. Blessed with a mild climate and delightful position close to the Alps, it attracts flocks of admirers to its shores and islands adorned with sumptuous villas and gorgeous ornamental gardens, a legacy of the late Renaissance when the commanding Visconti and Borromeo families were at the height of their powers.

In spite of its denomination *maggiore* ('greatest'), this is not Italy's largest lake, as Garda pips it to the post. Maggiore's perimeter runs for 170km and its surface area is 212km$^2$; however, its 66km length makes it the country's longest lake. The lake's western shore belongs to the Italian region of Piemonte, the eastern section is in Lombardia, while the top fifth is Swiss territory. Beyond the justifiably popular lakefront is a charming string of age-old alpine-style villages dotted over densely wooded mountain slopes and linked by ancient mule tracks and

*Sasso del Ferro from the Stresa waterfront (Walk 1)*

paths. Walks galore! Moreover, three of the countless mountains edging the lake are simply sensational belvederes. The Mottarone, Monte Carza and Sasso del Ferro are climbed on Walks 2, 8 and 12 respectively.

## EXPLORING THE LAKE

The main road SS33 and the Milan–Domodossola railway line travel north from **Arona** on the southwestern shore to the pretty village of **Belgirate**, conclusion of Walk 1. A quiet stretch of wooded shoreline continues to **Stresa** (Tourist Office tel 0323 31308 www. stresaturismo.it, www.visitstresa.com). 'I'm up here at Stresa a little resort on Lake Maggiore, one of the most beautiful of the Italian Lakes,' wrote Ernest Hemingway in 1929. Not everyone was so lucky as not long afterwards, in 1943, in the wake of Italy's racist laws, Jewish families awaiting safe passage to neutral Switzerland were deported.

Without a doubt Stresa is the most-visited town on Lago Maggiore – and with excellent reason. Apart from its beautiful waterfront lined with magnificent *belle époque* villas surrounded by immaculate parkland, it boasts easy access to the trio of world-famous Isole Borromee: Isola Bella, Isola dei Pescatori and Isola Madre. These tiny gem-like islands are jam-packed with exquisite gardens and villas. Charles Dickens wrote (1844), 'For however fanciful and fantastic the Isola Bella may be, and is, it still is beautiful.'

As well as plenty of ferries, frequent trains on the main Milan–Domodossola line stop at Stresa, while SAF buses provide a link with Verbania and a shuttle service for Milan's Malpensa airport. The many accommodation options include Hotel Elena (tel 0323 31043 www. hotelelena.com).

From the Lido di Stresa, also referred to as Carciano, a cable car (scheduled for re-opening in 2024) swings inland up the gently sloping Mottarone, an alpine belvedere *par excellence* with a breathtaking panorama. Walk 2 explores the mountain, while Walk 1 takes a stroll through the woods south of Stresa.

The next location of interest is **Baveno**, a quiet lakeside location served by SAF buses and ferries across to the islands and Verbania. Walk 2 concludes here (Hotel Beau Rivage tel 0323 924534 www. beaurivagebaveno.com).

After Baveno the lake shore swings into the delta of the River Toce at Fondotoce, a nature reserve. Campsites abound such as Campeggio Lido Toce (tel 0323 496220 www. campinglidotoce.eu). This rectangular body of water is often referred to as the Borromean Gulf, after the islands. Monte Orfano, a curious lump of granite explored in Walk 3, dominates the landscape here. The railway line then curves northwest and calls in at Pallanza-Verbania station, where Walk 3 begins, before proceeding to Domodossola. A VCO bus transports

Isola Bella

passengers from the station to Pallanza proper and other parts of Verbania.

**Verbania** is the name for the whole of the promontory but there are several ports of call, all served by ferry and SAF and VCO buses. The first is **Suna**, a nice place to stay a short detour off the busy main road (Hotel Pesce D'Oro tel 0323 504445 www. hotelpescedoro.it). Walk 4 starts here. A short drive above Suna stands the pretty village of **Cavandone**, reached on Walk 4 as well as by VCO bus.

Next and closest to the point is **Pallanza** with a Tourist Office (tel 0323 503249 www.verbania-turismo. it), pedestrian district, waterfront lined with magnificent magnolia trees, and plenty of hotels. It makes an excellent base. There's also a Youth Hostel (tel 0323 501648 www.ostelloverbania.

com). Pallanza is well served by ferries which shuttle across to the Borromean islands. Just around the point to the north is renowned Villa Taranto with its simply magnificent gardens (www. villataranto.it).

**Intra** acts as the port of call for the mid-lake car and passenger ferry across to Laveno and ferries from all over the lake. It is also an important terminal for SAF services from Stresa and beyond, as well as the VCO bus that runs from Domodossola and north to the Swiss border and Brissago. Intra has an interesting old town and makes an excellent base for visiting this central part of the lake, with plenty of good restaurants and places to stay. A kiosk (tel 348 2547482) near the ferry wharves acts as the tourist information point.

*A ferry arrives at Cannero Riviera (Walk 7)*

The SS34 narrows rather as it passes through **Ghiffa**, a modest line-up of shops and houses on the lakefront, which acts as the key gateway for the Sacro Monte Sanctuary route (Walk 5).

On a rounded promontory of fluvial deposit jutting out onto the lake, **Cannero Riviera** is set off the main road and boasts a decent, albeit shingle, beach (campsite Camping al Lido tel 0323 787148 www.campinglidocannero.com). The lakefront promenade is a line-up of inviting restaurants and elegant upmarket hotels. Handy for the bus stop is peaceful, family run B&B Casa al Mulino (tel 0323 787197 www.casaalmulino.it), while grocery shops and the friendly Tourist Office (tel 0323 788943 www.cannero.it) are a

short way downhill. Walks 6 and 7 start at Cannero Riviera.

Utterly charming **Cannobio** has a long pedestrian lakefront, which is especially animated of a Sunday for the weekly market that draws crowds from far and wide. Set off the road, the village has a historic heart with paved alleys and elegant *palazzi* as well as a well-stocked Tourist Office (tel 0323 71212 www.procannobio.it). Accommodation options include centrally located Hotel del Fiume (tel 0323 70192 www.hoteldelfiume.it). Walks 8 and 10 begin here.

Branching west from Cannobio is the beautiful wild **Val Cannobina**, which snakes its tortuous way up to join Val Vigezzo. It is explored in Walk 9; there is B&B accommodation at

Orasso (Pensione Belvedere tel 0323 77136 www.belvedereorasso.it).

Infrequent VCO buses reach the villages, but at rather inconvenient times for walkers, so the Cannobio taxi service (tel 392 5692728 www.ladolcevitacannobio.it) may come in handy.

Immediately north of Cannobio and Brissago, the top end of the lake enters Swiss territory, curving northeast to Locarno, and is not explored in this guidebook. On the other side of the water, not far south of the international border, the SS394 runs through the township of **Luino**. This town has good ferry links across to the western shore and Cannobio and Cannero, as well as rail links with Switzerland and south via Gallarate to Milan. While it somehow lacks the charm of the Piemonte villages, its great draw is the Wednesday market, when the whole town is invaded by long lines of stalls and huge numbers of shoppers who flock here for bargains. Luino is handy for Walk 11 as the Baldioli bus to Curiglia starts out from here. Hotels include Hotel Del Pesce (tel 0332 532379 www. hoteldelpesce.it), and there's a helpful Tourist Office (tel 0332 530019 www.vareselandoftourism.it, www. comune.luino.va.it).

The next useful place is **Laveno**, 16km south of Luino, linked to Intra by the mid-lake passenger and vehicle ferry. A modest spot with a good Tourist Office (tel 0332 543546 www. stradasaporivallivaresine.it), it is the gateway to the Sasso del Ferro mountain (Walk 12) and its curious *bidonvia* open-sided cable car that runs daily March–November. This town also hosts a bustling weekly market (Tuesdays), a legacy from the days when Laveno was the centre of the cereal trade. Accommodation is available at Hostaria del Golfo (tel 0332 666975 www.hostariadelgolfo. com). Trains on the Trenord line from Milano Cadorna terminate here.

## MAPS

The 1:50,000 Kompass map n.90 'Lago Maggiore' is fine for general orientation and planning, and covers all the routes except Walk 3. However, it

*The old part of Cannobio (Walk 7)*

*The Baveno waterfront*

is lacking in local detail, so use a local map where possible.

A decent 1:30,000 map of the paths around Stresa (useful for Walks 1 and 2) can be downloaded from www.stresaturismo.it. Tourist Offices including Luino and Laveno in the Province of Varese can provide the free 1:35,000 map 'Via Verde Varesina' Istituto Geografico De Agostini, good for Walks 11 and 12.

For Walks 6, 7, 8, 9 and 10 there's the Cartine Zanetti 1:30,000 sheet n.58 'Cannobio, Cannero Riviera' on sale locally.

### TRANSPORT

- Baldioli buses tel 0332 530271
  www.baldioli.it
- CTPI buses tel 0332 530271
  www.CTPI.it
- Ferry timetables tel 800 551801
  www.navlaghi.it
- Italian state trains tel 892021
  www.trenitalia.com
- Laveno cable car
  tel 0332 668012
  www.funiviedellagomaggiore.it
- SAF buses tel 0323 552172
  www.safduemila.com
- Trenord tel 02 72494949
  www.trenord.it
- VCO buses tel 800 503001
  www.vcotrasporti.it

# WALK 1
*Stresa to Belgirate*

| | |
|---|---|
| **Start** | Stresa Tourist Office, Piazza Marconi |
| **Finish** | Belgirate railway station |
| **Distance** | 9km (5.6 miles) |
| **Ascent/Descent** | 300m/270m |
| **Difficulty** | Grade 1–2 |
| **Walking time** | 2hr 40min |
| **Access** | Stresa can be reached by train and is well served by ferries which moor at Piazza Marconi alongside the Tourist Office. From Belgirate, trains back to Stresa are approximately hourly, more frequent than ferries. VCO buses can also be used. |

A string of old pathways, possibly of ancient Roman origin, link the lovely town of Stresa with quiet Belgirate, a little-visited lakeside village to the south. Signed as VL2 with red/white CAI waymarks that needs to be followed carefully, it passes through divine chestnut woods, with clearings offering inspirational lake views. The chestnut fruit was once fundamental to this area's economy and is referred to as *arbul* – in the local dialect 'the tree' – *par excellence*. Harvesting the nuts and maintaining man-made terraces is a thing of the past now, but plenty of reminders can still be seen along the way. This is an easy and very enjoyable half-day walk, with a return to Stresa either by ferry, train or bus.

Before setting out arm yourself with a snack as there is nothing in the way of cafés until Belgirate.

From lakefront Piazza Marconi and the **Tourist Office** (200m) at **Stresa**, go L (SSE) away from the town along the water's edge as far as the café Pasticceria Gigi. Here turn R on Via Rosmini (red/white waymarks) in gentle ascent past houses and a church, then go L on Via al Castello past houses. This becomes a paved path alongside a stone wall and joins a cobbled way in ascent to a cluster of houses.

*The lakefront at Stresa*

At an intersection with a shrine, fork L on Via Vecchia per Passera, a shady cobbled lane leading SSE into woodland along the boundary of the Villa Pallavicini gardens. It narrows to a good path, accompanied by a stream, and climbs steadily, maintaining the same direction. Further along, a house or two is passed and a minor road crossed, then it's up to a wonderful belvedere at the **Oratorio di Passera** (314m), a modest church erected in the 1700s by a local wine merchant to give thanks for deliverance after being shipwrecked on the lake. A quiet surfaced road leads on, with beautiful views to the opposite shore and the Sasso del Ferro mountain above Laveno.

A path takes over through chestnut wood to an abrupt veer R that has you puffing up steps. At a road go L down past houses and a playing field to the picturesque church and cemetery **Sant'Albino** (380m, 1hr 20min). Continue ahead for a beautiful section on a wide path through ancient chestnut trees, old terracing and huge fallen boulders. At a junction with a shrine, keep L as per the red/white signs and onto a lane through to a terraced

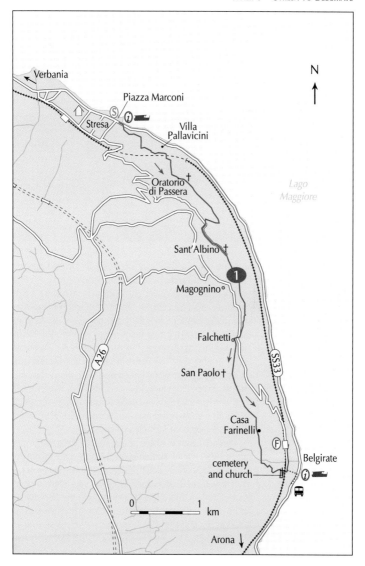

*On the way to Belgirate*

vineyard. Here a path leads up across a road and into the tiny hamlet of **Falchetti** (405m) in a scenic spot.

Gentle ascent leads past turnoffs (including 12th-century chapel **San Paolo**) before wide curves mark the start of the descent at last, in the company of chestnut trees and streams. Open fields allow views to the lower lake and the vast line-up of moraine ridges. A minor road leads through the **Casa Farinelli** (380m) intersection and on to a bridge crossing – then you fork sharp L as the path resumes its stepped way. Down at a road turn R and almost straightaway L at a shrine. A flight of steps concludes at the cemetery and Romanesque frescoed church, which boasts an elegant belltower.

Keep L past the church entrance for steps under the railway line. For the **station** go L now but for the lakefront, follow VL2 heading down another stairway. Keep R on Via Elena Conelli, curving S to where you need stepped Via dell'Imbarcadero that delivers you to the ferry wharf and Tourist Office of **Belgirate** (230m, 1hr 20min). The bus stop is a short stroll R.

# WALK 2
## *From the Mottarone to Baveno*

| | |
|---|---|
| **Start** | Stresa cable car, Lido di Stresa |
| **Finish** | Baveno ferry wharf |
| **Distance** | 15km (9.3 miles) |
| **Descent** | 1300m |
| **Difficulty** | Grade 2+ |
| **Walking time** | 3hr 50min (+ 20min for lift rides) |
| **Access** | Lido di Stresa aka Carciano is a 15min waterfront walk from the centre of Stresa, and ferries call in here. The *funivia*/cable car station is next to the wharf. Baveno at walk's end has frequent ferries back. |
| **Note** | At the time of writing the cable car was not operating due to the tragic 2021 accident. Plans are underway for a new lift to open in 2024. |

The route begins with the popular mechanised ascent, a memorable experience thanks to the spectacular vistas over lake and Alps. It's advisable to purchase the combined cable car/chair-lift (*funivia/seggiovia*) ticket all the way to the top. The walk is a very long descent but there's plenty of variety in terms of landscape and terrain, with woodland and pasture. The day concludes at utterly charming Baveno. From here you catch a ferry back to Stresa via those fairy-tale islands Isola dei Pescatori and Isola Bella that you've been admiring all day. Meals and refreshments are available at the top of the Mottarone as well as at the Alpino cable-car station halfway down, while an Agriturismo eatery is located at Alpe Cristina, in an especially panoramic spot (check opening times with the Tourist Office in advance).

If the complete walk looks too long for comfort, take a variant: either conclude at Alpino and the botanical garden (http://giardinobotanicoalpinia.altervista.org), well worth a visit, or ride the cable car from Stresa to Alpino and start there by following the detour to pick up the main route for Baveno.

From **Lido di Stresa** (200m) the cable car makes a spectacular lakeside departure on its two-stage trip to the **Mottarone station** (1378m). A chair lift climbs the final

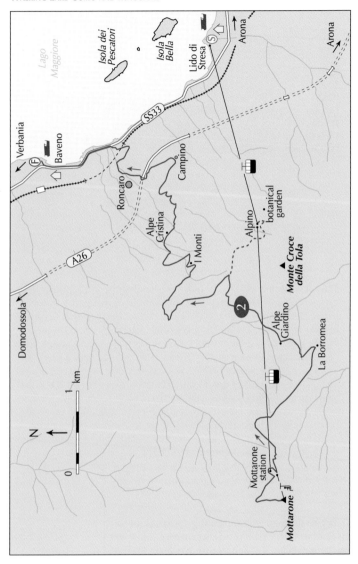

## THE MOTTARONE

The mountain called the Mottarone is invisible from the famous resort town of Stresa, largely because your attention is naturally drawn to the lake, busy with motor boats ferrying visitors around the pretty islands. However, rising above is a sprawling mountain that peaks some distance inland. Isolated between Lago Maggiore and Lago d'Orta, it is one of those apparently nondescript yet extraordinary lookouts that takes your breath away, especially if you're lucky enough to be there when the cool north wind is blowing, sweeping all trace of cloud from the alpine line-up, allowing multi-peaked Monte Rosa to stand out in all its glaciated glory. Also a modest winter ski resort, the Mottarone can be accessed almost year-round by a two-stage cable car, successor of a 1911–1960s cogwheel railway with electric traction, the original route of which is followed during the walk.

*On the summit of the Mottarone*

leg to the actual 1491m top of the **Mottarone** where an amazing panorama awaits.

> In optimum conditions a huge **360° arc of the Alps** can be admired, starring Monte Rosa to the west and pyramidal Monviso in the distance to the southwest. Closer at hand, at your feet, is Lago d'Orta, with Varese to the east.

From the summit cross, take the stony path N down grassy slopes bright with gentians, heather and blueberries. Rowan trees line the way as you reach a lane and turn R for the cable-car station and hotel/restaurant Eden (1378m, 15min).

A large yellow sign for path L1 'Sentiero Stresa–Mottarone' points you down a lane, keeping L of the cable-car station, with gorgeous views N to the light

*The Verbania peninsula and the renowned Borromean islands from the descent*

grey crests of the Val Grande beyond Verbania. The path passes under the cables for the first of several times, and heads down into conifer and mixed woodland, home to hundreds of songbirds. It's stony underfoot – watch those ankles. You're guided by occasional red/white and L1 waymarks, and all the junctions are clearly marked.

A long straight stretch SE with a constant gradient is clearly recognisable as the old cogwheel train line, rails long removed. At times the way is sunken with embankments, at others it is built up. A clearing close to the surfaced road corresponds to the former station of **La Borromea** (981m, 45min). Here L1 veers L (NW) on a more leisurely earth-based track through beech woodland. Abandoned houses stand at **Alpe Giardino** (960m) on the edge of a tall dark conifer wood.

Down through clearings you reach a lane and turn R (still NE) beneath the cable car again and past yellow poles for the underground *metanodotto* (gas pipeline). At a T-junction fork L and follow the lane as it circles Monte Croce della Tola and joins a wider level lane at a rusty metal bar (40min).

If you are interested in going to Alpino, then fork R here as follows.

### Detour to Alpino

The lane leads SE through wood, gradually dropping to horse-riding farms, a modest café-restaurant, the renowned Alpine Botanical Garden and the cable-car station of **Alpino** (800m), with great lake views. Allow 10min in descent or 30min in the opposite direction.

---

At the rusty metal bar go L, as per red/white waymarking for M5. A leisurely level stretch runs through silver birch, which soon thin out for superb views over Lago Maggiore and to the Verbania peninsula. Where you encounter the *metanodotto* (gas pipeline) the lane veers R and down to a junction overlooking the Toce delta and the beautiful sharp granite peaks of the Val Grande. Turn R (SE) towards pasture and groups of old rural buildings (**I Monti**), and onto a minor surfaced road. Not far along you need to fork L (signed for Baveno) through woods for 10min. At the next lane branch R through to the stunning position of the Agriturismo L'Ordin restaurant at **Alpe Cristina** (630m), an amazing place with spectacular views over the renowned Borromean islands, Verbania and the north end of the lake.

An old path lined with stone walling plunges through beautiful beech woods dotted with old huts. Look carefully for red/white waymarks at the junctions, and you'll soon reach the first buildings of the pretty, peaceful village of **Campino** (390m, 1hr 10min).

At a drinking tap branch L down steps through old houses and take Via A Stoppani to the church. Go L across the road to a sign for Baveno, and take the lane Via Madonna della Neve, which is lined with shrines. It reverts to a lane in woodland and curves close to a tunnel, quickly left behind. Through a residential area now, the way continues diagonally downhill, ducking below a house and into woods once more where old cobblestones reappear. This ends at a road where you turn R to quiet **Roncaro** (260m). Near the church fork L down Via Roncaro, a paved lane leading to the main lakeside road SS33. Go L and it's not far to pick up the beautiful lakeside promenade into charming **Baveno** (200m, 1hr).

# WALK 3

*Monte Orfano and Lago di Mergozzo*

| | |
|---|---|
| **Start/Finish** | Pallanza railway station |
| **Distance** | 13km (8 miles) |
| **Ascent/Descent** | 600m/600m |
| **Difficulty** | Grade 2–3 |
| **Walking time** | 4hr |
| **Access** | The railway station for Pallanza on the Milan–Stresa–Domodossola line can also be reached by regular VCO buses linking it with Pallanza and the rest of Verbania. Mergozzo is an alternative entry point – buses on the VCO Domodossola–Verbania run stop at the lakefront piazza. If arriving by car, park either near the railway station or at Montorfano. |

This walk is a fascinating circuit that touches on the historical military constructions of the Linea Cadorna – see Introduction – and follows many perfectly graded tracks of clear military origin from that time. The summit of Monte Orfano is a belvedere *par excellence*, not to mention a superb spot for watching birds of prey. The woods, on the other hand, are home to colourful jays and noisy nutcrackers.

It's a nice variation to detour to Mergozzo and its eponymous lake – or use the tracks as alternative access/exit. In any case, take plenty of drinking water and picnic supplies. You could always plan on dropping in to Mergozzo for refreshments, although you may not get there until mid afternoon.

From the **Pallanza railway station** (199m) walk down the road past a pink house to a car park close to the SS34 and a quarry. At the sign for Montorfano fork R on the quiet road, past store yards, to climb gently L (NW). After a couple of bends you pass the A56 path (the return route from Mergozzo). Keep on past the cemetery and up to **Montorfano** (334m, 30min), which boasts an exceptionally handsome Romanesque church.

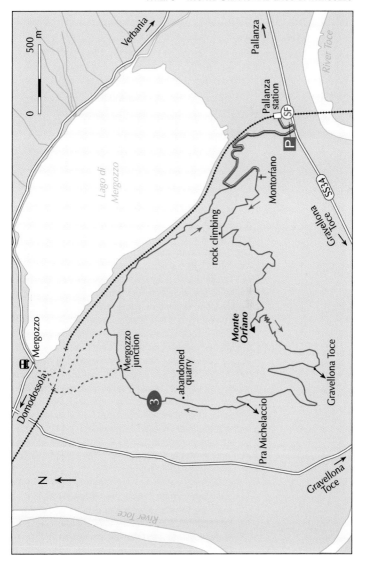

39

## MONTE ORFANO, MONTORFANO AND MONT'ORFANO

Monte Orfano – as the name suggests – is an 'orphaned mount', a mass of granite that separates tiny Lago Mergozzo from the River Toce which flows down the Ossola valley and into the Borromean Gulf and Lago Maggiore close to the Verbania promontory. The district has been renowned since medieval times for its prized marble and white and green granite, which was in great demand and fashioned into columns for churches in Rome such as San Paolo fuori le Mura. Even as late as 1830 Monte Orfano boasted 39 quarries, a handful of which are still operating today.

Be aware that the village on the eastern flank of the mountain is called Montorfano (also spelt Mont'Orfano), which can be a little confusing.

Without entering the village, take the signed path A56 which branches R; remnant patches of asphalt suggest it was once a road. As it curves W through the wood, gaps in the foliage offer views over Pallanza to Monterosso, then soon to Lago di Mergozzo.

Heading NW, the path becomes an atmospheric old military track with a perfect gradient through chestnut woods and with plentiful red/white waymarks. After curving L past a rock-climbing area, it reaches a level stretch with fallen rocks. The way narrows here and you need to clamber over several slabs. Further up, the path follows a curious long ramp that concludes at excellent lookouts over the River Toce to the Mottarone W. After a series of grassy terraces with silver birch trees then oak, pass a radio mast to come across surprisingly vast military structures connected with the Linea Cadorna, including underground premises and fortifications.

At a signposted junction go R for the actual flat *cima* (summit) of **Monte Orfano** (794m, 1hr 15min), marked by a stone pillar on an outcrop.

Not a bad spot for a picnic, this **belvedere** dominates the Ossola valley, running northwest and backed by glaciated alpine peaks, the fork southsouthwest to Lago d'Orta, the stark crests of the Val Grande standing out to the north, and Lago

Maggiore, with Stresa and the islands. No wonder it was considered strategic for the military!

Return to the signposted junction and fork R on the A58 (sign for Mergozzo) for the start of a remarkable military track – innumerable zigzags SW on a stone-edged path in almost imperceptible descent through chestnut woodland. Very slow progress in terms of descent, but at least it is kind on the knees! Ruined stone buildings are dotted along the way, and a broad saddle thick with gorse and ferns is passed. Soon the path veers sharp R down to a signed fork where you ignore the turn-off L for Gravellona Toce and keep straight ahead. The road-width track heads N at first before a long swing SW and past another turn-off (to Pra Michelaccio). A little further on, soon after a small abandoned quarry, take care not to miss the red/white-marked fork R off the lane for a clear path through old chestnut allotments. It's not far down to a couple of gnarled chestnut trees at the key **Mergozzo junction** (216m, 1hr 30min).

Unless you opt for the detour, go R (E) here, and you're soon joined by the return path from Mergozzo.

*Lago di Mergozzo and the River Toce from the ascent*

*The view from Monte Orfano embraces the Gridone and the Alps*

**Detour to Mergozzo (15min)**

From the junction, go L to a shrine marked for 'Mergozzo Lago'. Follow red/white waymarks carefully through lanes and alleys, over the railway line, past a tiny church and finally R downhill (past Via Montorfano/Sentiero Azzurro, the alternative access route – see below) to lakeside Piazza Cavour, with cafés and the bus stop at **Mergozzo** (196m).

To rejoin the main route, from the bus stop in Piazza Cavour on the lake's edge, go R (SW) up Via G Borzoni, then immediately L on Via Nostrani. Continue up to where a stepped cobbled way, Via Montorfano aka Sentiero Azzurro/A56, branches L. Not far along, at a shrine, ignore the fork for Oriola and keep on past houses into woodland. An old path lined with stone walls leads to the main route.

---

Leading SE is a beautiful paved lane with benches for admiring Lago di Mergozzo. A delightful stroll, above the railway line as well, it climbs gently to meet the road to Montorfano (30min). Now fork L down the tarmac to return to the **Pallanza railway station** (199m, 15min).

# WALK 4

*Cavandone on Monterosso*

| | |
|---|---|
| **Start/Finish** | Suna bus stop at the ferry wharf |
| **Distance** | 8.5km (5.3 miles) |
| **Ascent/Descent** | 265m/265m |
| **Difficulty** | Grade 1–2 |
| **Walking time** | 2hr 30min |
| **Access** | Suna gets frequent SAF buses on the Stresa–Verbania run as well as VCO buses linking Domodossola with Verbania. Few ferries call in. Cavandone is served by VCO bus from Pallanza. |

This pleasant loop walk crosses the southern flanks of Monterosso, the mountainous outcrop that dominates the promontory of Verbania halfway up Lago Maggiore. Old mule tracks with intricate paving and remarkably intact drystone walls are followed. The highest point, Cavandone, has superb views over Lago Maggiore and the surrounding mountains. The original layout of this pretty village is still evident: narrow streets and alleys lined with splendid *palazzi* constructed during the 1700s. It boasts a permanent (albeit small) population (including dozens of cats), and merits an exploratory wander.

Suna has plenty of restaurants, cafés and grocery shops, but there is nothing to eat at Cavandone so stock up on picnic supplies before setting out.

From the bus stop at **Suna** (200m), walk along the lovely lakeside to the church of Santa Lucia. Here turn R (CAI sign for route A00) up Via Solferino. This pedestrian alley leads past shops to Via dei Partigiani where you go L through the old part of the village, with arched courtyards and shuttered houses. You soon take a *sottopassaggio* (underpass) to duck beneath the main road in the company of the Rio Molinaccio stream. Turn L along Via XX Settembre then branch L again on Via del Buon Rimedio, a narrow surfaced way NW. Lined by high stone walls

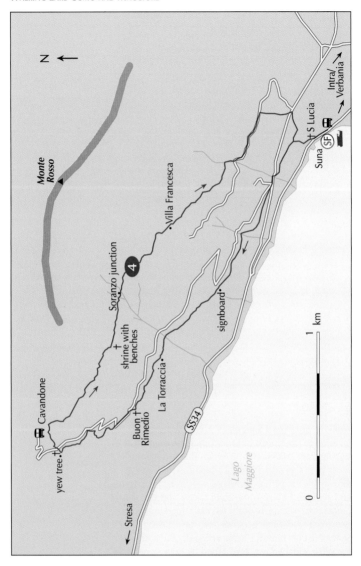

and rock faces, it climbs peacefully past well-kept homes shaded by huge trees and lush gardens overflowing with jasmine and roses. There is occasional red/white waymarking.

Where a road climbs R, you keep straight ahead on a paved path in gentle ascent through beautiful parkland and woods thick with honeysuckle. A wooden bridge precedes **La Torraccia**, a marvellous medieval tower that overlooks the Borromean Gulf; unfortunately it is private property but can be admired from behind a fence. The path becomes marginally steeper and features a couple of erratic boulders deposited there long ago by glaciers. It's not far to the disused 18th-century **Buon Rimedio church** in a clearing with great views across to the Mottarone, not to mention Stresa and the Borromean islands.

From the building it's only a matter of metres along the tarmac road then the old way resumes, passing orchards. A string of old shrines dot the way up to the 12th-century Chiesa di Cavandone, with a stupendous **yew tree** believed to be 600 years old! ▸

Cross the road and take the flight of steps past a huge walnut tree, into the old village. At a frescoed shrine fork R on the paved alley Via del Torchio to an oil press (*torchio*), then continue up to a well in a tiny pretty square in

Such trees were evidently originally planted at burial places by ancient peoples such as the Celts, to protect the dead.

*On the way to Cavandone*

*The* torchio *press in Cavandone*

**Cavandone** (455m, 1hr 15min). Do take time out for an exploratory wander through this charming village.

As signed, fork R (E) on Via Sardegna past an especially elegant palazzo from the early 1700s. Leaving Cavandone behind you head along a panoramic lane into woodland alternating with fields lined with stone walls. After a shrine with benches comes a brief uphill to the **Soranzo** junction (493m) – continue straight ahead (marked P01C). An unusual concentration of glossy green cherry laurel bushes accompanies the way.

After a stream crossing, the path descends decidedly, reaching a lane near houses, and a sign announcing **Villa Francesca** (394m). Go L on P01C to where the path resumes near a gated property. Passing old stone huts it plunges into the valley of Rio Molinaccio, finally emerging at tarmac. Here go L to join a wider road then soon sharp R for knee-challenging flights of steps. An underpass leads onto Via Mario Bobbio then it's R along Via dei Partigiani to where you branch L down Via Solferino as per the ascent route. You quickly reach the **Suna** lakefront (1hr 15min).

# WALK 5

*Ghiffa Sanctuary Loop*

| | |
|---|---|
| **Start/Finish** | Ghiffa bus stop at the ferry wharf |
| **Distance** | 10.5km (6.5 miles) |
| **Ascent/Descent** | 565m/565m |
| **Difficulty** | Grade 1–2 |
| **Walking time** | 3hr |
| **Access** | Ghiffa is on the VCO bus line between Verbania and Cannobio, and occasional ferries call here. Cars can be driven as far as the Sacro Monte sanctuary. |

The walk described here is an easy loop that takes in the peaceful Sacro Monte before wandering through the woods and embarking on a panoramic traverse back to the sanctuary. Easy lanes are followed the whole way (Grade 1), with the exception of the climb from the Sacro Monte up to the crest, only marginally more difficult (Grade 2). There are café-restaurants at the Ghiffa lakeside, Ronco and the Sacro Monte. The area is also a special nature reserve, taking in the eastern flanks of Monte Cargiago.

## THE SACRO MONTE OF GHIFFA

In the 15–16th centuries, fanned by a burning desire for a 'New Jerusalem', a curious religious fashion – to recreate scenarios from the Bible – swept across the alpine foothills of Piemonte and Lombardia. Life-size statues depicting the time of Christ, Mary and the saints populate scale reproductions of locations from the Holy Land. Rather kitsch to modern eyes, the 'Sacro Monte' (holy mountain) installations continue to be places of meditation and pilgrimage as well as venues for village fairs. The Sacro Monte of Ghiffa was constructed in full Baroque splendour during the 1700s, and is included in the group of nine awarded World Heritage status by UNESCO. Modest shrines also dot the mountainside and woods, and act as handy landmarks for walkers. www.sacromonte-ghiffa.com.

From the bus stop close to the ferry wharf at Ghiffa (198m) walk NNW (Cannero direction) along the promenade.

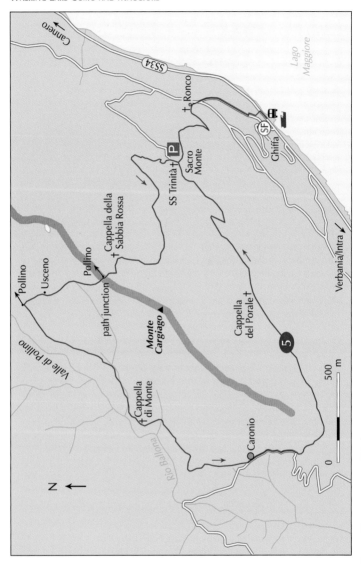

*Ghiffa sanctuary overlooks the lake*

Very shortly you need to cross the road L to take the stepped alley Via Volta alongside the PT (post office). There are faded signs for '*percorso pedonale*' (pedestrian route). The path winds uphill passing houses and walled gardens, continuing L on Via Motti to a road. Here fork R past old-style Hotel Paradiso and up to the panoramic village of **Ronco** (280m) and a café-restaurant.

Straight over the road take the flight of steps, keeping L past the cream façade of Chiesa della Visitazione. Another L will see you on the alley Via Torino (sign 'Al Santuario'). Soon turn R up Via Careghetta past gardens, keep R at a Y-junction and onto a shady lane. Climbing steadily, this enters pine and chestnut woodland. Ignore the fork R, and keep straight on for the **Sacro Monte sanctuary** aka **SS Trinità** (380m, 30min).

Four chapels, a colonnaded walkway adorned with plaster reliefs that acts as the Via Crucis, and terracotta statues can be admired at the **sanctuary**, along with lake views. Close by are car parks, café-restaurant and a toilet block.

From the uppermost car park and a map board take path n.18, which climbs N at first. Faded red/white waymarks on rocks and trees lead you up to a path junction to fork L on n.18. Not far along, n.18 branches R (W) as a path that climbs steadily. Ignore the link for Porale, and keep upwards, more and more steeply through beautiful chestnut woodland to the shrine, **Cappella della Sabbia Rossa** (640m). It dates all the way back to 1690 and still boasts a fresco, albeit faded and fragmented. Not far uphill from here you gain the wooded ridge from Monte Cargiago and a **path junction** (715m, 45min). Don't branch R for Pollino but go straight ahead on n.18b, which leads in gentle descent N to a clearing and the huts of **Usceno** (695m) for a wider track through to a major lane, n.1 in Valle di Pollino.

Branch L (SW), accompanied by the Rio Ballona stream and plenty of songbirds, via the **Cappella di Monte** shrine (600m). Keep on down to a road and branch L through the quiet village **Caronio** (494m), which enjoys views to the Mottarone behind Stresa as well as Lago Maggiore. At a sharp curve R in the road, at a traffic mirror, fork L, signed for the Santuario della Trinità. Buildings are quickly left behind on this absolutely beautiful stretch heading NE, a level stroll amid scented broom and myriad Mediterranean flowers and bushes, with fantastic views across the glittering lake. It's a gentle descent and you eventually enter cool conifer forest with **Cappella della Porale** (470m). Further along the lane are picnic tables, then the **SS Trinità** (380m, 1hr 15min) once again.

As per the ascent, fork R down the steps and back to **Ronco** and then the lakeside at **Ghiffa** (198m, 30min), with ferry wharf and bus stop.

# WALK 6

*Villages above Cannero*

| | |
|---|---|
| **Start/Finish** | Cannero Riviera bus stop |
| **Distance** | 16.5km (10.3 miles) |
| **Ascent/Descent** | 800m/800m |
| **Difficulty** | Grade 2 |
| **Walking time** | 4hr |
| **Access** | Cannero Riviera is served by frequent VCO buses; the bus stop is on the main road 5min from the lakefront, where ferries call in. Trarego has a VCO bus service, which is handy for a variant exit. |

This very rewarding circuit walk begins as a lakeside promenade around the fluvial fan that hosts Cannero Riviera, then climbs gently through a series of villages, each with characteristic stone-roofed buildings, and even the occasional stately villa. After the belvedere of Oggiogno, the path drops through woodland. Once Rio Cannero has been crossed the old gentle way resumes to Trarego. Located on the south-facing flanks of the Monte Carza–Pian Bello line-up, it is one of the rare inhabited mountain villages that still boasts a grocery store and bus service.

There are modest café-restaurants at both Oggiogno and Trarego, otherwise buy a *panino* beforehand at Cannero. All the villages have drinking fountains.

From the bus stop at **Cannero Riviera** (197m) turn downhill on Via Dante Alighieri. At the lakeside promenade (the ferry wharf is a short distance to the left) go R past a marina and campsite, then along the shingle beach. Keep L past a café and onto a path following the water's edge. At the end fork R up to the road near Hotel Rondinella. Taking great care with the traffic, follow the road L for a matter of metres to steps R (sign for Cassino). You bear L below a house to the start of an old paved mule track

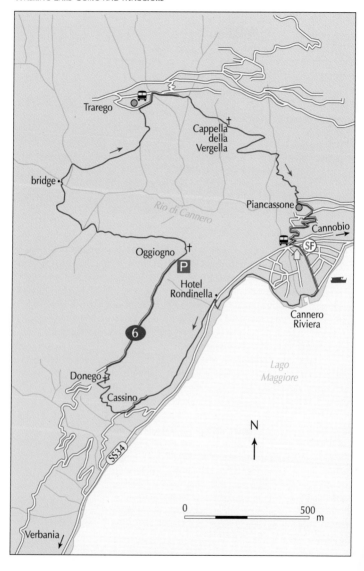

Trarego

Cappella
della
Vergella

bridge •

*Rio di Cannero*

Piancassone

Cannobio

SF

Oggiogno

P

Hotel
Rondinella •

6

Cannero
Riviera

*Lago
Maggiore*

Donego

Cassino

N

↑

SS34

0          500
                   m

Verbania

SW dotted with shrines. Accompanied by gorgeous lake views it reaches peaceful **Cassino** (45min).

An alley leads to the church, where you branch R on a cobbled path. Tight zigzags NW enter woodland then cross a surfaced road, to pass through an area of landslip where path and road have been reconstructed. With occasional red/yellow waymarks, you soon reach **Donego** (420m, 20min), a tranquil tiny hamlet, its *osteria* (bar) long closed. Fork R to the belvedere and church with a shady portico and stone benches. Not far along is a drinking tap where you need to fork L under an ancient arch at house n.26. Steep, well-worn steps cut into the

*Oggiogno is overshadowed by Cima di Morissolo*

53

Set on a dramatic outcrop in the shadow of triangular Cima di Morissolo to the west and Monte Carza to the northeast, the village is a superb lookout.

rock. Further up fork R along the quiet road and stick with it to **Oggiogno** (515m, 30min), a favourite summer haunt of swifts. ◄

Walk past the car park and through to Piazza dei Terrieri alongside the church, where elegant villas and gardens flank a jumble of old stone-roofed dwellings. Turn L down the alley with the gushing fountain, and past simple eatery Agriturismo La Rondinella. Next comes an amazing *torchio* (wine press) dated 1742, fashioned from a single chestnut tree. Go L here on Via per Trarego. It's not far to another fountain then a sign for n.10 for Trarego, a wide path heading NNW into chestnut woodland with some huge trees.

After a ruined house and a stream is a path junction where you keep R, as per blue paint splashes, for a zigzagging plunge down a steep wooded slope. At the bottom is heavy-duty steel netting close to the **bridge** (548m) which crosses Rio di Cannero high over a dramatic ravine. Red/white waymarking takes over for the leisurely ascent on a good path via a sequence of terraces and stone huts in chestnut woods. A field edged by cherry trees is reached and a lane leads up to a path junction – go R on a minor road on the lower edge of **Trarego** (796m, 1hr 20min) with its neat gardens and cottages. ◄ Keep on to the road intersection and bus stop.

For the village centre and café, fork left up any alley.

A short distance R is the signed path junction where you fork R for Cannero. A lane leads through an arch and past a couple of houses to a gigantic chestnut tree. Then porticoed **Cappella della Vergella** marks the start of a lovely paved descent SE. It curves this way and that, with plenty of views to Cannero below and Luino on the opposite shore. Down at **Piancassone** you join the road from Trarego at a bus stop. A short way downhill fork R on a surfaced minor road with red/white waymarking, an older version of the road to Trarego. It concludes down at the main road near the bus stop at **Cannero Riviera** (197m, 1hr).

# WALK 7

*The Cannero–Cannobio Traverse*

| | |
|---|---|
| **Start** | Cannero Riviera ferry wharf |
| **Finish** | Cannobio ferry wharf |
| **Distance** | 8.5km (5.3 miles) |
| **Ascent/Descent** | 420m/420m |
| **Difficulty** | Grade 1–2 |
| **Walking time** | 2hr 20min |
| **Access** | Cannero Riviera and Cannobio are served by frequent VCO buses linking Verbania with Brissago. In both cases the bus stop is on the main road 5min from the lakefront, where ferries call in. |

This justifiably popular walk links the two charming villages of Cannero Riviera and Cannobio, both set on the northeastern shore of Lago Maggiore, just short of the Swiss border. Easy lanes and paths leave walkers free to delight in the many belvederes over the lake. One highlight is beautiful car-free Carmine Superiore, founded in the 10th century as a fortress, and its stunning Romanesque church.

There are no refreshment points en route so be self-sufficient. The return trip to Cannero Riviera can be made by either bus or ferry.

From the ferry wharf at **Cannero Riviera** (197m) walk to the nearby northern end of the promenade and go L up Via Massimo d'Azeglio. Then it's R under an arch (sign for Nordic Walking), past a tiny harbour and up a stepped lane diagonally R between houses n.6 and 7 (while the Nordic walkers keep L). A jasmine-draped alley wanders by lush gardens and villas in enviable locations. The main road is crossed to a paved stepped way that climbs gently ENE to a leisurely panoramic level stretch touching on gardens, the odd house and swathes of chestnut woodland.

Keep straight on at the hamlet of **Cheggio** (281m) to pass a house in a fantastically scenic location that takes

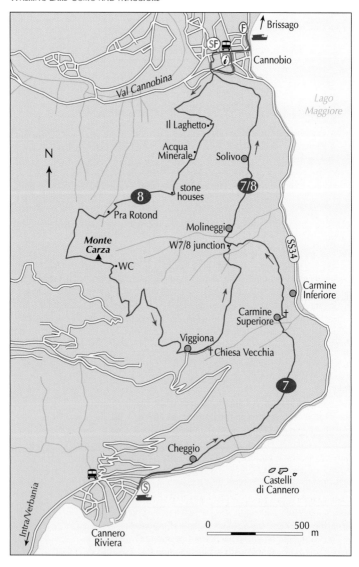

in the curious 12–14th-century Castelli di Cannero-cum-islands below. A wider paved track winds uphill into chestnut woodland, where massive boulders dot the undergrowth. After a dried-up pond and short descent, ignore the turn-off R for Carmine Inferiore. A little further on, curve across a side stream to a stone bridge and keep R into charming **Carmine Superiore** (305m, 1hr). Detour R or you'll miss the Chiesa di San Gottardo – what a gem!

*The path climbs away from Cannero Riviera*

> The tiny houses of Carmine Superiore, with old slab-tiled roofs, occupy a prominent rock outcrop overlooking the lake. Pride of place goes to the exquisitely frescoed Romanesque **Chiesa di San Gottardo**, dating from the 1300s, which has a welcoming terrace. The hamlet has only a handful of residents, who share the unique atmosphere with clouds of alpine swifts.

Follow the rocky alley-cum-high street down to a flight of steps and across a succession of streams. You touch on a road then take steps for a steady drawn-out uphill path. ▶

As the way levels out look out for trenches amid the trees, heritage of the Linea Cadorna (see Introduction).

*Leaving Molineggi*

After a waterfall comes the final climb that concludes at a **junction** (30min) with the path from Viggiona and Walk 8.

Turn R across the cascading stream and through **Molineggi** (454m), with its beautiful lake views and old water-powered mills, many of which are now holiday accommodation. Follow the lane in descent, with long paved sections. At a ramp with a barrier (L) keep straight ahead on a pedestrian way with red/white markings. After a short stretch of asphalt go L through rural properties (**Solivo**); only minutes along, don't miss the fork L for a lovely old path. With superb bird's-eye views to the photogenic Cannobio waterfront backed by the Swiss Alps, it leads down to the residential area where you are directed R. Down at the main road cross over and take Via alla Campagna, which becomes Via Roma. Then go R on Via A Giovanola to the belltower. Here keep L past the Tourist Office to reach the bus stop on the main road at **Cannobio** (220m, 50min).

For the ferries, proceed straight ahead on Via Umberto I to the lakeside, and go left for a host of inviting cafés not far from the ferry wharf.

# WALK 8
*Monte Carza*

| | |
|---|---|
| **Start/Finish** | Cannobio bus stop |
| **Distance** | 17km (10.6 miles) |
| **Ascent/Descent** | 900m/900m |
| **Difficulty** | Grade 2–3 |
| **Walking time** | 5hr |
| **Access** | Cannobio is served by frequent VCO buses linking Verbania with Brissago on the Swiss border. Many ferries also call in. The main bus stop is outside the principal church on the main road; the ferry wharf is 5min away on the lakefront. |

A superb day out on Monte Carza, the easternmost extremity of the rugged mountainous ridge that delimits Val Cannobina and overlooks Lago Maggiore. Added historic interest comes in the shape of trenches belonging to the Linea Cadorna (see Introduction).

The walk follows old paved tracks and clear paths through beautiful woodland en route to the summit belvedere, which arguably rates as the best on upper Lago Maggiore. The ascent is rather long but problem-free; the height gain puts off many people, and you will probably have the mountain to yourself. Only after Viggiona during the return will other walkers keep you company as a stretch is shared with the popular Cannero–Cannobio traverse (Walk 7). Take plenty of liquid refreshment and food as there are no cafés en route, although many hamlets during the descent have drinking fountains.

▸ From the bus stop outside the church at **Cannobio** (220m), turn S (in the direction of Verbania) along the main road (SS34, Via Uccelli). At the nearby intersection fork R at the sign for Val Cannobina. It's not far along to a clutch of signposts and a map board where you keep L then follow signs for Monte Carza, soon parting from the Viggiona/Cannero route. The road narrows quickly

See map for Walk 7.

through houses and gardens, with views north to the village of Sant'Agata below Monte Giove. As the tarmac comes to an end, a path breaks off L and begins a steady well-graded climb SW through woodland past derelict buildings. Further up you reach a lane and go R to where the path resumes. At the sign announcing **Il Laghetto** (little lake, 495m) – and with no water in sight! – branch L and soon rejoin the lane in ascent. Keep your eyes peeled for the many shortcuts.

At a field and farm signed **Acqua Minerale** (590m) ignore the detours for the impossible-to-find 'mineral water' spring. Ahead you encounter two stone houses at a path junction. Fork L away from the buildings through dense beech woodland, but quickly veer R (WSW) and not far along you will be rewarded with a decent view down to Cannobio and the lake, thanks to the swathe of trees that have been cleared for power lines. Further up a stream is crossed and the trees thin, opening up a vast panorama to the northern lake and Switzerland. Then you reach the summer farm **Pra Rotond** (940m, 2hr), set amid flower-filled meadows.

Now gird your loins for the final slog SSW. The path finally emerges on the upper ridge and a lane with a brilliant panorama. Go L for **Monte Carza** (1116m, 30min). The summit is a veritable carpet of broom and ferns, with wide-ranging views from Cannero to Luino on the opposite shore and the southern lake. ◄

*For fantastic views north to Switzerland, make a short detour downhill left to the radio mast.*

The path continues E to a rather old portable **WC** (!) sitting on the edge of the Linea Cadorna with a trench system. Turn sharp R here (SSE) to a chapel and panoramic picnic area. The red/white route soon forks L in common with a mountain bike (MTB) trail. Watch your step on the loose stones. From bracken and heather the path moves down to a copse of silver birch. After a pylon, you leave the mountain bike route and fork R down through chestnut woodland to a concrete lane at the entrance to a property. Go L in descent to a fork (a short distance from a surfaced road), and L again along to a track intersection at a house – sharp R here sees you traverse a hollow thick with narcissus. Follow waymarks carefully SSE past old

stone huts and huge chestnut trees and into the attractive village of **Viggiona** (693m, 1hr 10min). Clear signs point down an alley to Piazza Pasquale which encloses the Chiesa di San Maurizio, shady benches and cool drinking water.

*A jumble of rooftops at Viggiona*

Go diagonally L on Via per Cannobio, lined with stations of the cross. You soon pass to the L of a cemetery and exceptionally beautiful Romanesque **Chiesa Vecchia**, which sports a vast slate roof. Now a paved way heads gently downhill through chestnut woodland, past more trenches of the Linea Cadorna and to a strategic **junction** (30min) on the Cannero–Cannobio traverse.

Go L across the cascading stream and through **Molineggi** (454m), with its beautiful lake views and old water-powered mills, now converted into holiday accommodation. Follow the lane in descent then go R on a signed path. A surfaced road is joined briefly, then you're signed L at **Solivo** for a lane through rural properties. Superb bird's-eye views of the photogenic Cannobio waterfront backed by the Swiss Alps are enjoyed. A path now leads down to the residential area traversed

*Chiesa Vecchia, Viggiona*

at the walk start. Keep R for the main road and back to **Cannobio** and the bus stop (220m, 50min).

The most rewarding way to conclude this fantastic walk is to stagger down to the lakefront for well-deserved refreshment, while gazing back up to Monte Carza towering above the village.

# WALK 9
## *Val Cannobina*

| | |
|---|---|
| **Start** | Orasso car park |
| **Finish** | Cannobio bus stop |
| **Distance** | 20km (12.4 miles) |
| **Ascent/Descent** | 700m/1150m |
| **Difficulty** | Grade 2 |
| **Walking time** | 5hr |
| **Access** | Orasso is served by sporadic VCO buses; you may need a taxi (mob 348 7821699). Spoccia, 1hr along, could be used as alternative access to shorten the day. Cannobio is on the VCO bus line between Verbania and Brissago on the Swiss border. Many ferries call in here. The bus stop is outside the principal church on the main road; the ferry wharf is 5min away. |

This absolutely wonderful full-day walk begins high up in Val Cannobina, 15km from Cannobio and Lago Maggiore. With the exception of a short stretch of tarmac between Gurrone and Cavaglio, it follows clear marked paths and paved lanes, crossing countless mountain torrents on elegant stone bridges and dropping in and out of the villages. The route is known as the Via Borromea for the pastoral visit of San Carlo Borromeo, archbishop of Milan in the 1500s, who travelled along it to visit his subjects.

The charming village of Orasso, set on lower Monte Torriggia, has the only grocery shop encountered today, alongside a café-restaurant. Cavaglio, a good three-quarters of the way down, has the only other café. **Note** Every village on this walk has a tap or fountain with drinking water. There is accommodation at Orasso (see Lago Maggiore Introduction).

▶ From the car park at the entrance to **Orasso** (700m) follow the red/white signs for Cannobio through the web of alleys past the ancient yet remarkably intact house Ca' du Vécc', with frescoes and a timber overhang. From the pretty church, its bell tower adorned with a sundial, is a superb view south to Monte Riga, dotted with stone

Orasso was named from the Latin oratio for 'prayer', and is the valley's oldest settlement, dating from the 1300s.

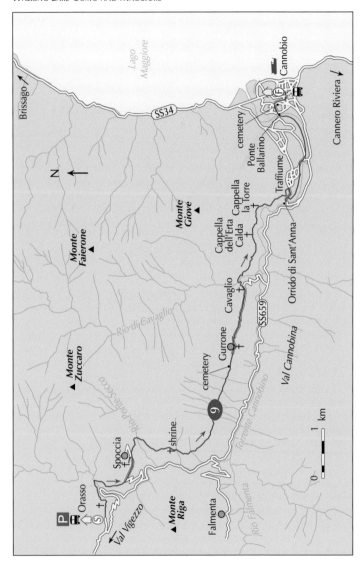

## VAL CANNOBINA

Val Cannobina is a rugged and densely wooded V-shaped valley, carved out by the eponymous torrent. Soaring above, the mountain fringes touch the 2000m mark. Their upper slopes are dotted with ancient alps, once summer pasture for livestock from traditional scattered villages, photogenic settlements of stone houses sporting tiny wooden balconies. In the face of limited opportunities for employment, and the downturn of the chestnut market due to competition from potatoes and cereals during the 19th and 20th centuries, the local population has dwindled from many thousands to just a handful today; for instance, Orasso shares a mere 120 residents with neighbouring Cursolo. Numbers do increase marginally in summer due to holidaymakers.

shepherds' huts. Heading NE the path narrows and enters woodland on its way down to the first lovely bridge and stream crossing. A gentle climb leads S to a shrine and a road where you go uphill to a path junction, and L again up to **Spoccia** (798m, 1hr). All but deserted, this picturesque hamlet is brilliantly located. ▶

Return the same way to the road and turn L uphill past the 'H' helicopter pad to the junction R for Gurrone.

From the war memorial look south towards Falmenta and Monte Riga; from the church gaze up to Monte Zuccaro.

*Spoccia and Orasso nestle in the woods in upper Val Cannobina*

*En route to Gurrone*

It soon passes terraces with a row of stone huts and crosses Rio Ponte Secco. The ensuing lengthy stretch, due S and level, has sections cut into the rock face. A **shrine** doubles as a brilliant belvedere to Monte Zeda to the southwest, back to Orasso and Spoccia, Monte Zuccaro and the knobbly Gridoni outcrops, as well as Monte Riga and scattered hamlets. The next watercourse boasts a lovely waterfall and an especially elegant stone bridge, and soon an orientation table puts names to all the mountains and villages far and wide.

Moving SE after a rocky point you pass two houses, then a water trough and a pasture clearing. Further on is

WALK 9 – VAL CANNOBINA

a **cemetery** and path junction – keep L uphill to join the road into **Gurrone** (700m, 1hr 15min). ▶

The tarmac takes you through to the church and a car park, where a handkerchief corner of glittering Lago Maggiore is now visible. Now follow the unappealing steep road downhill ESE to **Cavaglio** (501m, 20min). Walk through the village, detouring to the bar/café if needed, as far as the church where drinking water is found at the foot of the bell tower. Soon you fork L where the old way resumes, an admirable piece of civil engineering as the mule track plunges in a succession of tight curves in easy descent to a majestic bridge high over Rio di Cavaglio.

The old way continues through shady woodland, soon forking L uphill to a stone column commemorating the fall of the mule bearing San Carlo in 1569. The path levels out en route to the **Cappella dell'Erta Calda**, fitted out with benches where wayfarers could rest. Val Cannobina has narrowed considerably now, and the descent soon begins in earnest, with plunging views to the riverbed below. At frescoed **Cappella la Torre**, now derelict, a toll would be exacted for the use of the road. You finally emerge on the road at **Traffiume**, and branch R to the dramatic ravine, the Orrido di Sant'Anna (250m, 1hr 30min) and its whitewashed church. The bridge here is said to date back to Roman times.

Take the stepped ramp down to the riverbed and pool, then follow the track for walkers and cyclists (*pista ciclopedonale*) E through the trees along the watercourse. After a road bridge keep on through fields to **Ponte Ballarino**.

It's worth taking time to explore this village, with its atmospheric covered passageways and wooden loggias.

*The riverbed below Orrido Sant'Anna*

*Ponte Ballarino*

This **bridge**, whose name means 'wobbly bridge', is a suspension bridge with a story to tell. In order to replace a precarious plank across the tumultuous stream (where people had been swept away), in 1933 villagers raised the money themselves to finance a bridge. Flood damage later put paid to that one, and the current version was built in the 1980s.

Once on the opposite bank (café), walk straight ahead along the minor road to an intersection and branch R to pass the concrete wall of the **cemetery**. At the car park, keep R as per the sign 'Centro Storico'. An alley leads through to Piazza Casnago then Via A Giovanola where you turn L. Ahead stands the elegant bell tower not far from the main road and bus stop of **Cannobio** (220m, 1hr).

If you have any energy left, wander on down to the lakefront for a well-deserved drink.

# WALK 10

*Cannobio–San Bartolomeo in Montibus Circuit*

| | |
|---|---|
| **Start/Finish** | Cannobio bus stop |
| **Distance** | 12km (7.5 miles) |
| **Ascent/Descent** | 450m/450m |
| **Difficulty** | Grade 2 |
| **Walking time** | 3hr 40min |
| **Access** | Cannobio is served by frequent VCO buses linking Verbania with Brissago on the Swiss border. Many ferries call in here. The bus stop at Cannobio is outside the principal church on the main road; the ferry wharf is 5min away on the lakefront. |

An absolutely delightful circuit with masses of natural and historical interest. Highlights are the isolated Chiesa di San Bartolomeo in Montibus and the string of delightful old mountain hamlets and villages set in beautiful woodland on the eastern slopes of Monte Giove and Monte Faierone, close to the Swiss border. A dense web of paved tracks has linked them since time immemorial, and the many alpine streams are crossed via dozens of tiny arched stone bridges straight out of a fairy story.

The excellent network of paths in this area served refugees and partisans during World War II. Stories abound of volunteers who put their lives at risk to help political and Jewish refugees escape to Switzerland, while there are tales of smugglers who exacted a stiff fee for their guiding

Numerous variations are possible thanks to links with the main road and bus stops, such as at Darbedo and San Bartolomeo. There are no cafés or shops, but several villages have working drinking fountains.

From the bus stop at **Cannobio** (220m) follow the main road SS34 N to cross the bridge over Torrente Cannobino. Fork immediately L on the *pista ciclopedonale* (track for cyclists and walkers) past Albergo del Fiume and picnic benches. Take the first fork R through to the road; a short way L is a map and signposts for the beginning of the

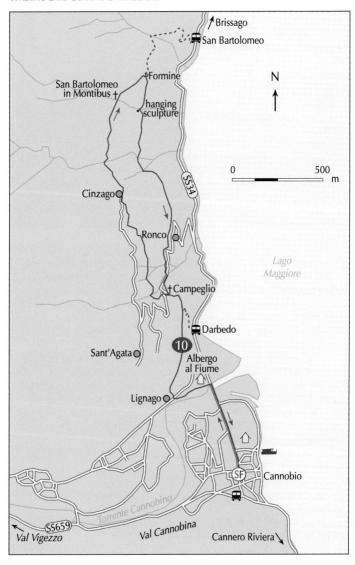

marked route at **Lignago** (20min). You puff up a steep cobbled ramp past houses to the path. Flanked by a wall smothered in honeysuckle that drenches the air with its perfume, the path moves off N, heading for woodland alive with birdsong. The first of the many dwarf stone bridges is soon encountered, a tad prior to a broad paved mule track from Darbedo on the main road.

Fork L here up to quiet **Campeglio** (351m, 20min) and its simple church. Waymarks point you up across the road; at a yellow house ignore the fork L for Sant'Agata and keep straight on a concreted lane. This transforms into a delightful wide woodland way in gentle ascent NNW across a sequence of stone bridges over cascading streams. At **Cinzago** (501m) you get a vast view over the northern reaches of Lago Maggiore to Locarno and Switzerland. The path wanders through the atmospheric village, almost a ghost town, with odd signs of renovation to the tall stone houses with their attractive wooden balconies.

You're soon back in woodland on your way N to the ancient **Chiesa di San Bartolomeo in Montibus** (523m), where twin chestnut trees shade benches fashioned from

*The church of San Bartolomeo in Montibus*

It is possible to follow a signed path northeast to reach the main lakeside road at the village of San Bartolomeo for the bus back to Cannobio.

mill stones. Now it's over another bridge and downhill via shrines to the close-packed jumble of stuccoed houses and well-kept vegetable gardens that comprise **Formine** (450m, 1hr 20min). ◄

At the tiny chapel, fork sharp R and thread your way down past houses, taking care not to miss the branch R (S). This quickly leads back into the woodland as a level path, crossing a curious ravine and a pool with a hanging sculpture. The path narrows and swings in and out of side valleys, a short stretch of cable acting as a handrail where there is marginal exposure. It's a non-stop sequence of pretty green glens with bridges, streams and stepping-stones to **Ronco** (315m, 40min). This delightful village boasts gorgeous lake views, elegant flower-bedecked villas, a church, and a resident sculptor whose amusing works are dotted around the alleys. Due S now it's past a goods lift and you join the road, turning R. Not far along you branch L through a car park and up to **Campeglio** (351m, 20min), past the church and up to the junction passed earlier on.

*Old and new houses make up Campeglio*

Turn L down the paved track and retrace your steps to **Lignago** and **Cannobio** (220m, 40min).

# WALK 11
## Monteviasco

| | |
|---|---|
| **Start/Finish** | Curiglia |
| **Distance** | 15.6km (9.7 miles) |
| **Ascent/Descent** | 800m/800m |
| **Difficulty** | Grade 1–2 |
| **Walking time** | 4hr (3hr 10min cable-car option) |
| **Access** | Curiglia, 15km from the lakeside, can be reached on the CTPI bus (Mon–Sat, line n.1) departing from Luino waterfront, a short stroll from the ferry wharf. Car owners should note that the road to Curiglia is particularly narrow and tortuous; park at the village or down at the cable car. |

An age-old mule track consisting of well over 1000 stone steps ascends for almost 400m. And where does it lead? A place where time stands still: Monteviasco, a unique, picturesque village, miles from the nearest road. It nestles in the alpine foothills of beautiful Val Veddasca, a pocket of Italian territory squeezed out of Switzerland. According to legend, four deserters from an occupying Spanish army took refuge here in the 16th century and built homes. Desirous of company, they successfully kidnapped some girls from Biegno on the other side of the valley. A delegation of furious men armed with pitchforks marched on Monteviasco but to no avail, as the victims were reportedly quite content to stay!

The walk commences with the marvellous mule track from Piero, near Curiglia – avoidable if you opt for the 10min cable-car ride to Monteviasco – and proceeds as a loop around the head of Val Viascola on clear paths and lanes. Curiglia has a grocery shop and café.

▶ From the bus stop below the church at **Curiglia** (666m) follow the *funivia* signs that take the L downhill fork of the road. It's possible to short-cut the first two bends in descent, then follow the tarmac NE along wooded Val Veddasca to the car park and cable car at **Piero** (549m, 30min). Immediately after the cables is the

The funivia/cable car was temporarily closed at the time of writing – check locally or plan to walk up.

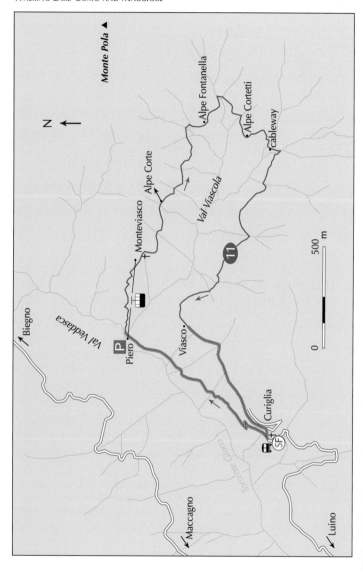

*Monteviasco spreads across the mountainside*

## MONTEVIASCO

While not exactly bursting at the seams with residents, the village seems to be doing notably better than similar alpine settlements that have road links. It is inhabited year-round by 20 souls, and even has a twice-weekly doctor's surgery. In 1991 a cable car was built to serve the tenacious inhabitants and get the kids to school on time. Nowadays, this remarkable oasis is a magnet for visitors, the majority of whom go to dine at the modest family-run trattorias serving fresh local produce and traditional specialties.

start (R) of the monumental mule track. A thousand or so perfectly graded steps climb due E up a wooded shoulder and past a handful of shrines. This is undeniably the most appropriate way to reach enchanting **Monteviasco** (926m, 1hr). The settlement looks west to the scattering of villages opposite, dotted over the steep wooded flanks

of Val Veddasca below Monte Cadrigna, and a corner of
Lago Maggiore can just be glimpsed.

Walk through to the church and its belvedere terrace, and take the paved street L with red/white waymarks. Keep L at the next junction, with an inviting
rustic restaurant, and L again at a shrine, thus leaving
the village. After a handful of working farms the path
is less trodden and the surrounds wilder. Heading ESE
you encounter pasture clearings, rapidly recolonised by
bracken and broom once abandoned. Ignore a turn-off
left for Alpe Corte and stick to the main path through
copses of silver birch and a string of ruined huts, many
of which have collapsed roofs. The path swings SE to
cross two cascading streams amid forget-me-nots and
alpenrose to reach the promontory of **Alpe Fontanella**
(1081m), the highest point on the walk. Here are superb
views over thickly wooded Val Viascola and beyond.
Behind, northeast, a rugged wooded crest marks the
border with Switzerland.

Handrails lead down to steps across two more cascading watercourses as you move to the southern side
of the valley and begin a gentle climb SW to the saddle
occupied by **Alpe Cortetti** (1048m, 1hr). The scattered
buildings of this sizeable, yet abandoned, hamlet, nest-
ling in divine rich green beech woodland, are immensely
evocative. Not far downhill is the first of several fords,
announced by a sign *guado*. In normal conditions the
stepping-stones are sufficiently high, although after heavy
rain you might get your boots wet. At the loading point
for a rusty goods cableway and hut, the way widens to a
level lane running WNW through gorgeous beech trees
to a corner outcrop where Monteviasco can be admired.

Evidence of charcoal burning and woodcutting is
clear en route to **Viasco** (873m), a cluster of dairy farms
on a prominent corner. A surfaced road takes over for
the rest of the way in descent SW to **Curiglia** (666m, 1hr
30min), and back to the bus stop.

# WALK 12
## Sasso del Ferro

| | |
|---|---|
| **Start/Finish** | Laveno ferry wharf |
| **Distance** | 8.5km (5.3 miles) |
| **Ascent/Descent** | 110m/850m |
| **Difficulty** | Grade 2 |
| **Walking time** | 2hr 30min |
| **Access** | Laveno is linked to Intra on the opposite shore of the lake by frequent vehicle and passenger ferries. It is also served by Trenord trains from Milano Cadorna. |

Standing out clearly on the central eastern shore of Lago Maggiore is imposing Sasso del Ferro, a mountain completely smothered in dark green woodland. Its great attraction is an old-style *funivia* cable car, more a *bidonvia* (rather like a string of metal buckets clanking their way upwards). It terminates at the 950m Poggio Sant'Elsa belvedere, easily one of the best on Lago Maggiore. The belvedere also doubles as a take-off platform for paragliders, and there's a popular café-restaurant. An optional extension goes to the 1062m top of Sasso del Ferro for a broader outlook over the hills of Varese.

The walk rates average in terms of interest; nearly all in descent, it spends much of its time in beech woodland, and touches on Casere, a cluster of houses with a renowned restaurant, before heading back down to the Laveno lakefront.

*The panorama stretches from Monte Rosa across the vast lake and the islands, as well as down to Varese.*

From the ferry wharf at Laveno (210m) turn L along the waterfront lined with plane trees. Stick with the main road curving R and follow '*funivia*' signs to the departure station (10min). Enjoy the super-scenic ride through the trees to **Poggio Sant'Elsa** (950m, 20min) and awesome views. ◄

Instead of heading immediately downhill, from the gliders' launching pad, turn uphill through woodland on the steep red/white-marked path. A little way up, follow the disused ski lift that will lead you directly to the top of **Sasso del Ferro** (1062m), alive with swallows. Visibility

*Laveno, overshadowed by Sasso del Ferro*

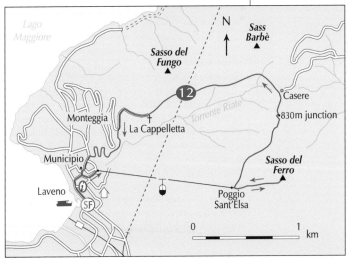

*A path sign on Sasso del Ferro*

permitting, the views here are 'limited' to the hills around Varese to the southeast, lower Lago Maggiore and the plains beyond.

Back down at Poggio Sant'Elsa (30min), take the path at the rear of the restaurant, signed for Laveno. It becomes a stony track running NNE through beech woodland, soon reaching a lane **junction** (830m, 30min) where you fork R. It's not far down to the saddle at Casere (750m). ◄

*Turn off R here for Ristorante Gigliola.*

A wide, renovated mule track now begins its long descent W high above Torrente Riate. Clearings allow glimpses of the lake and Laveno. At a shrine, **La Capelletta** (520m), are a couple of houses and a café.

Now the way is surfaced and quite steep at times. At the houses of **Monteggia** (at the sign for Brena), fork off the road onto a concreted lane. Later, tarmac takes over on a quiet but knee-testing road through a residential area. At a T-junction with pastel-stuccoed buildings, turn L along an old road with paving stones (Via Caprera) then R on Via Tinelli into Piazza Fontana and the Municipio palazzo. Here fork L on stepped Via Palestro, continue downhill towards the church and go L along the lakefront past the Tourist Office to the ferry wharf of **Laveno** (210m, 1hr).

# LAGO DI COMO

A paved street winds downhill through delightful old Naggio (Walk 19)

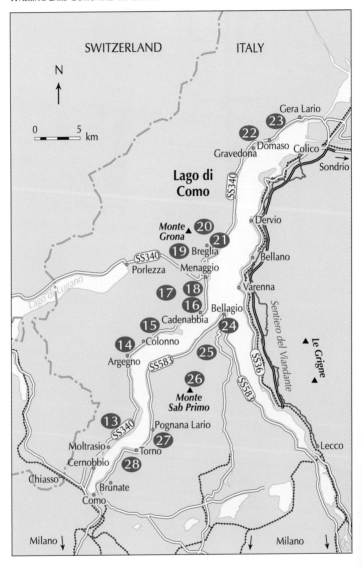

# INTRODUCTION

'This lake exceeds anything I ever beheld in beauty, with the exception of the Arbutus Islands in Killarney. It is long and narrow, and has the appearance of a mighty river winding among the mountains and forests,' declared Shelley in 1818, while William Wordsworth wrote (1793).

> How bless'd, delicious Scene! the eye that greets
> Thy open beauties, or thy lone retreats;
> Th' unwearied sweep of wood thy cliffs that scales,
> The never-ending waters of thy vales.

Ever magnificent, the splendours of Lago di Como were also broadcast by the likes of Pliny and Strabone back in ancient Roman times. Today Italians inevitably associate it with the great writer Manzoni, whose landmark novel *I Promessi Sposi* (*The Betrothed*) begins there; the heroine Lucia shares her name with the traditional Lago di Como rowing boat. Overseas visitors are attracted by the breathtaking scenery and romantic atmosphere, augmented by the host of villas and superb gardens – not to mention the

*Sala Comencina and the lower lake (Walk 15)*

glamour of international celebrities such as George Clooney, who has a home there.

An upturned 'Y' in shape – rather like a tuning fork – the 146km² expanse of Lago di Como is wholly in Lombardia. It is fed mainly by the River Adda, which flows in from broad Valtellina, recipient of glaciers and snowfields from the mighty Bernina and neighbouring Alps. And as it spreads southwards it is split into two branches by the spectacular Bellagio promontory. The Adda chooses the southeastern arm and leaves the lake at Lecco, flowing on to swell the waters of the River Po. Curiously, there is no river exit at Como, at the end of the southwestern arm, so the town is vulnerable to flooding. These days it is rare to see the city barricaded against rising water, but back in the 1300s it was common, and blamed fairly and squarely on the Milanese Visconti dynasty, who constructed bridges at Lecco that substantially narrowed the watercourse, thereby obstructing flow.

The 16 day routes and five-day trek described here will show that the area has much to offer walkers. Lago di Como is strategically placed in relation to the Alps; trade routes known to the Celts and Etruscans between Switzerland and the southern plains logically intersected here, meaning that modern-day walkers often tread in centuries-old footsteps.

## EXPLORING THE LAKE

In the south **Como**, the centre for the Italian silk industry, is a convenient and especially lovely place to stay. Its pedestrian-only centre is graced by an exquisite Romanesque cathedral and a host of outdoor eateries and cafés on the water's edge (Tourist Office tel 031 269712 www.visitcomo.eu). Stay at good value Hotel Quarcino (tel 031 303934 www.hotelquarcino. it), Hotel Marco's (tel 031 303628 www.hotelmarcos.it) or the Youth Hostel (tel 031 570889 www.ostello bello.com). Good ferry services commence here. Como has two railway stations: located 5min uphill from the waterfront is San Giovanni-Como for the main line trains from Milano Centrale that continues via Chivasso

*The Como–Brunate funicular (Walk 30)*

*The wonderful gardens of Villa Carlotta look across the lake to Bellagio (Walk 15)*

into Switzerland. The other belongs to Trenord, and is located close to the lake's edge; this has runs to Milano Nord Cadorna where there are Metro connections to Milano Centrale. ASF buses start out at Como to serve the lake's western shore: all stops to Menaggio and then to Colico at the head of the lake.

One of Como's great attractions is the marvellous funicular railway constructed in 1894. Walk 28 begins with the ride. It still trundles almost vertically to the hill retreat of **Brunate**, where the wealthy would escape the summer heat of the plains in the privacy of elegant villas surrounded by shady pine and beech woodland. It is still a nice place to stay and doubles as a superb lookout for admiring Torino and the Monviso on a clear day. Sleep at Vista Lago (tel 031 364070 www.hotelvistalago.it) or at Albergo Paradiso (tel 031 364099 www.hotelparadiso como.com) at San Maurizio.

From Como the narrow road SS583 hugs the eastern shore on its way to Bellagio, served by an ASF bus. It passes through a string of picturesque waterside villages, including **Torno**, the conclusion of Walk 28 (stay at Hotel Vapore tel 031 419311 www.hotelvapore.it), then **Pognana Lario** where Walk 27 begins. High above towers the vast Triangolo Lariano, the mountainous peninsula separating the Lecco and Como arms of the lake, perfectly triangular in shape (as the name implies). It is dotted with glacial erratics, huge rock chunks broken off distant mountain flanks where the glacier once flowed, and carried for miles to be deposited far from their original geological context. Several can be admired during Walks 27 and 28.

The northernmost tip hosts picture-perfect, world-famous **Bellagio**, bang in the middle of the lake, beautifully located on a promontory that divides Lago di Como in two – its name means 'two lakes'. And Punta Spartivento, its northernmost extremity, 'divides the wind' that comes rushing down from the Alps and doubles as a lovely lookout. The town attracts a chic 'want-to-be-seen' crowd, who come in the hope of

*Villa 'La Quiete' at Bolvedro near Tremezzo (Walk 15)*

spotting the rich and famous in sleek motor launches or lounging in luxuriant villa gardens. Hype apart, it is a wonderful place to spend any length of time, but be aware that accommodation and restaurants do not fall into the budget category (Tourist Office tel 031 951555 www.promobellagio.it).

Bellagio has excellent passenger and car ferry links with Varenna on the eastern shore and Cadenabbia and Menaggio to the west. Lecco Trasporti runs buses to and from Lecco; for taxis tel 335 6299588. Walk 24 explores the surrounds of Bellagio, Walk 25 from nearby Guggiate aims for the Monte Nuvolone lookout, while Walk 26 climbs to superb Monte San Primo, the highest point on the Triangolo Lariano. Accommodation possibilities include Hotel Centrale

(tel 031 951940 www.hc-bellagio. com). At nearby Pescallo is Hotel La Pergola (tel 031 950263 www. lapergolabellagio.it).

From Como the SS340 heads along the western shore via **Cernobbio** with its outstanding villa. Not far along is quiet **Moltrasio**, where Vincenzo Bellini composed inspired arias for his opera *La Sonnambula* during his sojourns. Walk 13 commences here, on its way to Laglio, further along the waterfront. Where the lake widens and curves northeast is **Argegno** with its council-run cable car that whizzes visitors and residents up to the rural peace of the mountainside village of **Pigra** for Walk 14.

Not far around is **Colonno**, which marks the start of Walk 15, the 'Greenway' that wanders parallel to the road all the way to Tremezzo and adjacent **Cadenabbia**. Here stands Villa Carlotta with lemon arbours and luxuriant beds of gorgeous rhododendrons (www.villacarlotta.it). It has frequent ferries, not to mention grand hotels lining the waterfront and even an Anglican church testifying to the erstwhile British community. Walk 16 begins here.

Unpretentious **Menaggio** is perfectly located for walks on the western side of the lake and is a good place for an extended stay to explore the surrounds thanks to excellent public transport on both land and water (Tourist Office tel 0344 32924 www.menaggio.com). Frequent passenger ferries call in from Bellagio and Como, as does the Varenna car ferry. ASF buses on the Como–Colico line are frequent, and local runs start here.

It has a good range of accommodation, including Ostello La Primula (Youth Hostel: tel 0344 32356 www.lakecomohostel.com), waterfront Albergo Bellavista (tel 0344 32136 www.hotel-bellavista.org). Away from the lakeside at Loveno is Hotel Loveno (tel 331 2827882 www.hotel-lovenolakecomoitaly.com), transit point for Walk 19, which climbs into Val Sanagra. Continuing a fair way uphill is the quiet village of **Breglia**, the start of Walk 20, which aims for Monte Grona and the neighbouring panoramic ridge, along with Walk 21 to the village sanctuary. A good bus service from Menaggio comes this far, and you can stay at Albergo Breglia (tel 0344 37250 www.breglia.it).

On the SS340 road west for **Porlezza** on Lago di Lugano is Croce with Hotel Adler (tel 0344 32171

*At Menaggio (Walk 19)*

www.hotel-adler-menaggio.it), a key landmark for the start of Walks 17 and 18.

Although the mountain slopes are more gentle along the shoreline of the upper western edge of the lake, the backdrop of the dramatic alpine line-up is more impressive. Visitors to this part of Lago di Como are fewer in number, so it's a quieter area to visit. Moreover, it has been dubbed the 'Little Tuscany of Lario' due to a wealth of exquisite Romanesque churches, exemplified by landmark black-and-white chequered Santa Maria del Tiglio on the lakefront at **Gravedona**. Served by ASF buses and ferries, this is the first town of interest to walkers and Walk 22 begins here, giving a good taste of this pretty district. Stay at Hotel La Villa (tel 0344 89017 www.hotel-la-villa.com) or Hotel Regina (tel 0344 89446 www. reginahotels.it). Gravedona has a lakefront Tourist Office (tel 0344 85005 www.visitgravedona.it).

Buses and ferries continue around to lakefront **Domaso** and the beginning of Walk 23 (Tourist Office tel 324 0914635 www.domaso.it). Rooms are available at Ristorante dei Pescatori (tel 0344 96088 www.ristorantedeipescatori.com) and Hotel Camping Europa (tel 0344 96044 www.hotelcampingeuropa.com), which doubles as a well-organised campsite.

It's only a short bus ride to the resort village of **Gera Lario**, where Walk 23 concludes, close to the mouth of the River Mera in an area beloved of windsurfers. Across Pian di Spagna the lake shore curves south to the huge River Adda and the town of **Colico**, the conclusion of the Sentiero del Viandante (see the trek description for accommodation listings). Roads and a coast-hugging railway run down to Lecco. Heading south, important train stops include quiet **Dervio**, an overnight trek staging point, where the occasional ferry pulls in. The village is set on a sizeable alluvial promontory formed by sediment carried by the river Varrone.

Next comes **Bellano**, once dubbed the 'little Manchester of Lario' for its wool and cotton mills, most of which stand empty and forlorn today. Its modern-day claim to fame is an awesome *orrido* (ravine) touched on during the trek.

The strategic mid-lake car ferry from Menaggio docks at charming **Varenna**, a good alternative base for visiting Lago di Como without the crowds often encountered on the western shore. Pastel-coloured houses and villas overlook an old harbour.

Further south and boasting a waterfront castle and even a small beach, is laid-back **Lierna** and its station. From there the next useful stop is **Abbadia Lariana**. Both have an attractive *passeggiata lungolago* (lakeside promenade) as well as good facilities for Sentiero del Viandante trekkers. Near the lower end of Lago di Como's eastern arm stands the town of **Lecco** with plenty of trains to Milan. This well-served town is where the trek

*Lucias: traditional lake boats*

begins its five-day adventure north. It is also considered the gateway to the climbing haven of the soaring Grigne mountains, which account for the eastern bulk of the lakeside.

(Walks 22 and 23) is covered by the 1:35,000 map 'Alto Lario Occidentale', published by the Comunità Montana Alto Lario Occidentale, and is on sale in the immediate area.

## MAPS

The Kompass 1:50,000 map n.91 'Lago di Como' covers all the walks and is adequate for planning, but the large scale precludes much detail. An excellent 1:25,000 *carta dei sentieri* (walking map) for the Triangolo Lariano and Walks 24–28 is available at local Tourist Offices, as is the 1:25,000 Comunità Montana 'Alpi Lepontine' carta topografica escursionistica for Walks 16–21 around Menaggio. The Menaggio office also has a simplified map downloadable from its website www.menaggio.com, as does the Bellagio Information Office on www.promobellagio.it. The upper lake

## TRANSPORT

- Argegno cable car
  www.comune.pigra.co.it
- ASF buses tel 031 247111
  www.asfautolinee.it
- Como–Brunate funicular
  tel 031 303608
  www.funicolarecomo.it
- Ferry timetables tel 800 551801
  www.navlaghi.it
- TreNord tel 02 72494949
  www.trenord.it
- Lecco Trasporti buses
  tel 0341 359911
  www.lineelecco.it
- Italian state trains tel 892021
  www.trenitalia.com

89

# WALK 13
*Moltrasio to Laglio*

| | |
|---|---|
| **Start** | Moltrasio ferry landing stage |
| **Finish** | Laglio |
| **Distance** | 5.2km (3.2 miles) |
| **Ascent/Descent** | 150m/150m |
| **Difficulty** | Grade 1–2 |
| **Walking time** | 1hr 45min |
| **Access** | Moltrasio can be reached by either ASF bus (line C10 or C20) or ferry from Como. The walk's end Laglio, on the other hand, just has buses (C10 or C20). |

This delightful walk explores a string of charming villages set in magnificent panoramic spots along the lower southwest edge of Lago di Como. Paved alleys and lanes are followed the whole way, making for straightforward walking, and where marvellous views can be enjoyed. There is plenty of drinking water available en route and the villages offer cafés and restaurants as well as grocery shops.

From the ferry landing stage close to the bus stop at **Moltrasio** (247m), turn L (Como direction) along the main road and past a monument to the composer Bellini, who often sojourned here. After the Grand Hotel Imperiale, turn R up the stepped way Via F Raschi, which follows a high stone wall. It is known locally as the 'scala santa' (holy staircase) for the religious processions that once came this way. You emerge near the Municipio and bear R past a huge, pale yellow church in Piazza San Martino. It's next L on stepped Via G Curié to Piazza Umberto 1°. Here go R past a slender yellow building and under a viaduct on Via G Bianchi, overlooking the entrance to an awesome cleft valley with a spectacular waterfall.

Up at a fork, ignore Via Molino and keep R to a minor road at **Tosnacco**. Cross over and continue up narrow panoramic Via G Bianchi past houses to an old *lavatoio* (wash trough) and fountain. Then it's straight ahead on paved alley Via G Marconi in gentle descent. Just before a car park, fork abrupt L on wide Via Linera signed for 'Strada Panoramica per Urio e Carate'. This leaves the houses behind and becomes a lovely quiet level stroll NE past gardens, affording marvellous views across the lake to Torno and the mountains.

As you reach houses above Carate Urio, continue along Via F Corridoni to the **cemetery** (45min). A minor road then leads L over an old stone bridge and it's straight ahead to **Cavadino** (325m) with its old but well-kept stone dwellings. Keep R at the next alley fork then L up Via 4 novembre. Not far along a bridge is crossed near an old quarry before the **Santuario Santa Marta**, with an elegant 12th century Romanesque church, cemetery and picnic tables.

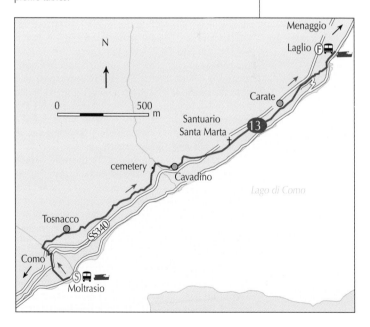

*The Santuario di Santa Marta is a lovely spot*

From here Via Santa Marta, lined with via crucis shrines, leads downhill to duck under the main road and descend past houses. Further down where tarmac is reached, a tad to the L is Via San Rocco. This narrows to a pedestrian-only alley through the houses of **Carate**. Follow Via Vittorio Veneto, then Via Olzavino NE parallel to the lakefront on a quiet, fascinating stretch in the shade of tall buildings with covered passageways and between walled gardens. The way curves R downhill at a small power pole. You need the first L, resuming the NE direction with gentle ups and downs on Via Piave.

Magnificent cypress trees line the way, which changes name to become Via delle Frazioni, part of upper Laglio. At a **car park** and houses keep straight on. Not far along, as the road curves R past a larger parking area, walk straight ahead for the paved alley heading downhill over a bridge and past houses with more covered passageways. At turn-offs stick with the wider alley (Via Soldini) fitted with a handrail. This comes out at the roadside, close to a tiny harbour. Turn L watching out for traffic. Only 5min away after the church at lakeside **Laglio** (240m, 1hr) is the *alimentari* (groceries) where bus tickets are sold. The bus stop is a few metres on.

# WALK 14
*Pigra to Colonno*

| | |
|---|---|
| **Start** | Cable-car station at Pigra |
| **Finish** | Colonno |
| **Distance** | 5.8km (3.6 miles) |
| **Ascent/Descent** | 50m/660m |
| **Difficulty** | Grade 2 |
| **Walking time** | 2hr |
| **Access** | Year-round buses on the C10 and C20 lines (ASF) stop at the lakeside cable-car station (*funivia*). Allow 5min for the cable-car trip up. Ferries call in at both Argegno and walk finish of Colonno, also on the C10 bus run. It's a 10min walk from the ferry and centre of Argegno (210m) to the cable car. The *funivia* usually departs every half-hour. |

Perched 600 dizzy metres above the southwestern edge of Lago di Como is the sleepy rural village of Pigra, where this superb route begins. A 12-passenger cable car, run by the local council for its residents (but open to anyone), gets you to the walk start. After this enjoyable mechanised ride, comes an old mule track with paved sections and superb views of the lake and the Alps. It drops into old rural settlements on a longish descent that can be knee testing at times, on its way back to the lakeside and Colonno.

The handful of small restaurants and cafés at Pigra are good for lunch or picnic supplies, otherwise there are facilities at Colonno.

Alight from the cable car at **Pigra** (859m) and once you've got your breath back head straight up the road past a café. Ignore the turn-off R for the Belvedere and continue in ascent on Via G Verdi past well-kept houses. After the Post Office it's the second L (still Via G Verdi and signed for Corniga), which climbs steeply to a crossroads near an old *lavatoio* (wash trough) and the Municipio. Branch R on Via Sociale, which terminates in a small square, giving

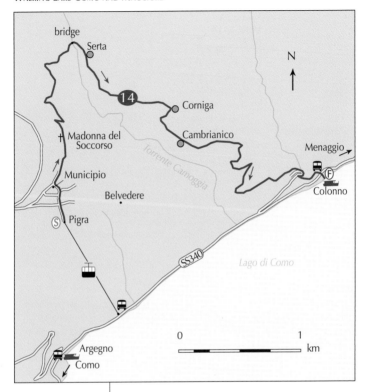

way to a clear lane heading N. Brilliantly panoramic, with views across Lago di Como to the Grigne mountains and Bellagio, it leads past the chapel of **Madonna del Soccorso**. Wide curves then descend gently through light woodland to a **bridge** crossing Torrente Camoggia in the valley of the same name.

A steep path climbs out the other side past a cluster of houses (**Serta**, 830m) then SE alongside a dry stone retaining wall on a lovely stroll to the mountainside hamlet of **Corniga** (760m, 50min), which has a handful of summertime residents. ◀

At the church detour briefly L to inspect the curious cylindrical stone construction that once served as a *nevera*, an ice store-cum-fridge for dairy products.

At the lovely porticoed church fork R (S) for the paved lane leading downhill out of Corniga to neighbouring **Cambrianico**. The lake views here are superb, but they get even better on the ensuing descent. Walkers may find this section knee testing, and rest stops provide a chance to admire the acrobatics of the occasional motorbike riders who urge their battered steeds up gravity-defying stretches to access their mountainside abode.

Down at tarmac in the upper residential area of **Colonno**, turn L down the road but soon L again on a concreted ramp giving way to steps between old houses (as per Greenway signs). At a broad alley, turn R downhill to where this burrows under the main road and continue to the lakeside and ferry landing stage. Otherwise, from the underpass take the steps to the main road and **bus stop** (tickets at nearby Bar Sport) at Colonno (200m, 1hr 10min).

Should you wish to proceed on the Greenway route, see Walk 15.

*The mule track descending towards Colonno affords wonderful views over the lake and to the Alps*

# WALK 15

Colonno to Cadenabbia on the Greenway

| | |
|---|---|
| **Start** | Colonno, Bar del Lago |
| **Finish** | Cadenabbia car park |
| **Distance** | 10.5km (6.5 miles) |
| **Ascent/Descent** | 100m/100m |
| **Difficulty** | Grade 1 |
| **Walking time** | 3hr 15min |
| **Access** | The C10 bus line (ASF) along the northwestern shore of Lago di Como calls in at Colonno – alight at the central bus stop outside Bar Los Molinos. Cadenabbia is also served by the C10 bus line, as well as ferries. |

Never straying far from the divine lakeside, the leisurely 'Greenway' drops in and out of the villages tucked off the main road (negligible ascent/descent). Several sections of the ancient Via Regina transalpine way are incorporated in the route, which is a combination of walkers-only lanes and paths and occasional surfaced roads. Buses and ferries call in at most of the lakeside villages, so you can do selected chunks and come and go at pleasure. Around halfway, peaceful Lenno has a smattering of waterfront eateries and cafés, although plenty more are encountered en route.

Steel lozenges embedded into the path show the way, as do blue/yellow arrows set at most key junctions. **Note** The official start (*inizio percorso*) of the Greenway is at the southernmost end of the village of Colonno, and to reach it entails a nerve-racking walk along a narrow stretch of busy main road. It is more logical and pleasant to begin the walk in the middle of the village, as described here.

From the bus stop in the vicinity of Bar del Lago in **Colonno** (200m) – with an eye out for passing traffic – walk in the direction of Como to cross a bridged stream. Very soon you go R down steps below the road level. Then turn immediately L up the alley to a path T-junction. Here are blue/yellow arrows for the Greenway, so go R. This leads through the fascinating old part of the village

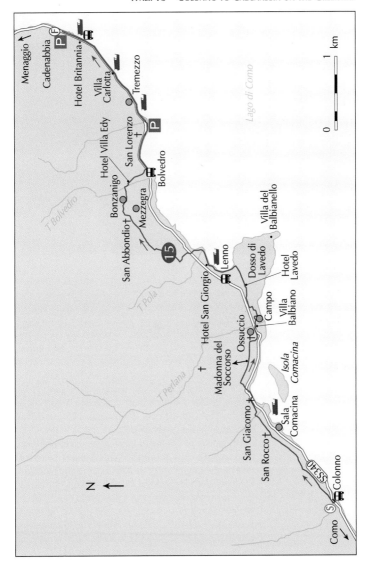

*San Giacomo stands on the lakeside*

Ignore the fork R *passaggio al lago* unless you need the village of Sala Comacina.

then gently ascends through vegetable gardens and orchards, flanked by stone walls. Isola Comacina comes into sight on the lake below, with an inspiring mountainous backdrop.

A level stretch goes above a newer residential area and a cemetery and past the yellow shrine of **San Rocco**, recognisable by the painting inside of the saint with a wound on his leg. ◀

A delightful cobbled lane descends gently amid olive and fig trees to the main road, which you need to cross for the tiny 12th-century Romanesque **Chiesa di San Giacomo** (40min): a pretty spot.

Continue on the path parallel to but below the road, then branch L on a pedestrian crossing and up steps past Osteria del Giuanin. Ignore the route for the sanctuary Madonna del Soccorso and fork R here along the tarmac to a square between the local school and a park. Proceed straight across at a roundabout and not far on turn R down Via Castelli to another admirable Romanesque church. Keep L of the building to reach the war memorial and bus stop on the road at **Ossuccio** (30min).

Cross over to Piazza Cardinale where you can peek through a railing to see stately **Villa Balbiano** with its ornate gardens. A pedestrian bridge leads over a river (Torrente Perlana) and into the atmospheric photogenic centre of **Campo**, once an ancient Roman settlement. Arrows point the way along its maze of alleys, past Villa Monastero, and back up to the road. It's not far to a caravan park and, further on, **Hotel Lavedo**. Continue in the same direction along the edge of a park with picnic tables, the inland edge of the wooded promontory **Dosso di Lavedo**, which belongs to Villa Balbianello (tel 0344 56110 www.fondoambiente.it), out of sight from here, but well worth a visit.

The lovely lakeside awaits, as you curve around to **Lenno** (30min), with inviting alfresco cafés and restaurants, not to mention a bus stop on main road. Past the ferry landing stage stick to the lakefront past Hotel San Giorgio and onto a shingle beach. At its end, an alley heads up to cross the road to a flight of steep steps. Turning R, it's onto a quiet road through a residential area, which enjoys vast views over Lago di Como. Just 5min along, keep diagonally L on cobbled Via Pola

*Along the waterfront at Lenno*

Vecchia and then Via G Brentano Mezzegra, which has a chapel. After the huge rococo **Chiesa di San Abbondio**, which stands out like a beacon and has lovely views to the Bellagio peninsula, you head downhill to the Municipio of Mezzegra, which occupies an elegantly ornate palazzo. An alley leads through the charming old village and a covered passageway below 17th-century Palazzo Rosati in **Bonzanigo** (270m).

With a great outlook east to the Grigne mountain range, fork down the tarmac way, lined with olive trees. Then go L along Via delle Gere, over a stream, R downhill and then L past **Hotel Villa Edy**. A paved alley leads down to the main road at **Bolvedro** and a bus stop (50min).

A promenade L along the water's edge passes marvellous stately Villa La Quiete, then the **Chiesa di San Lorenzo**. Go R and duck into the beautiful grounds of the civic park on the lakefront, with aged shady trees and a fountain. It's a popular spot for picnics and even swimming.

It's not far now along the pavement past the ferry wharf of **Tremezzo** to superb **Villa Carlotta** and its magnificent stepped gardens, a must-visit (tel 0344 40405 www.villacarlotta.it). The Greenway proceeds through **Cadenabbia** (201m) past the magnificent façades of grand hotels, another ferry wharf and bus stop opposite Hotel Britannia, before coming to its official conclusion after the minuscule Lido beach, at a car park (45min). ◄

*The vicinity of traffic along this section tends to encourage walkers to bail out earlier.*

*Steel lozenges embedded in the path show the way*

# WALK 16
## San Martino Circuit

| | |
|---|---|
| **Start/Finish** | Cadenabbia (Griante), Hotel Britannia |
| **Distance** | 5.7km (3.5 miles) |
| **Ascent/Descent** | 250m/250m |
| **Difficulty** | Grade 2 |
| **Walking time** | 2hr 30min |
| **Access** | Cadenabbia can be reached by ferry; from the wharf, turn right along the road to Hotel Britannia. Otherwise, catch a C10 bus (ASF) and get off opposite the hotel. |

This delightful circuit leads to the little church and sanctuary of San Martino that clings to the sheer cliff face high over the lake: a peaceful spot where visitors can drink in a far-reaching panorama and enjoy the tranquillity. The church is of great symbolic importance to the local population as it is home to a precious 15th-century statue of the Virgin and Child that miraculously found its way up here, ostensibly without human help! The paved path leading up to the church is lined with shrines and votive statues, and is both steep and stepped but not difficult.

The return path loops through woodland and passes rural properties before joining an old way that descends to the bustling lakeside.

From **Hotel Britannia** at **Cadenabbia** (201m), turn away from the lake on Via Roma. Only minutes up at a church, take the flight of steps (Via Mazzini) up to Via Brentano where you turn R past the **Municipio** (Town Hall), then L as you reach the **war memorial**. This street passes a park with an ancient beech tree before curving R to a T-junction at a yellow house with a ceramic Madonna and child. Branch R under an arched passageway and proceed along the alley (Via Tommaso Grossi) through the old district to reach Piazza **San Rocco** and its church. Keep R here on narrow Via San Martino, looking over to where the tiny white church is perched on the mountainside. After bearing L on tarmac you quickly reach the signed fork R for steps down to a **bridge** across a stream. Heading essentially NW, the path, lined with vegetable gardens, follows the stream. Soon a long series of paved and stepped ramps climbs endlessly through pretty woodland. Votive shrines are dotted along the way, and there's a small chapel too – all a good excuse to get your breath back!

At a **path junction** (446m) fork R still in the company of shrines. Not far along, just past a **bench**, is the fork L for the return loop. But for the moment continue on past a *Caduta Massi* (rockfall) warning sign and across a gully on a lovely rock path with a handrail NE for the last panoramic leg to the **Chiesa di San Martino** (475m, 1hr 15min): a simply stupendous spot. The building appears to be clinging to the cliff edge – needless to say there

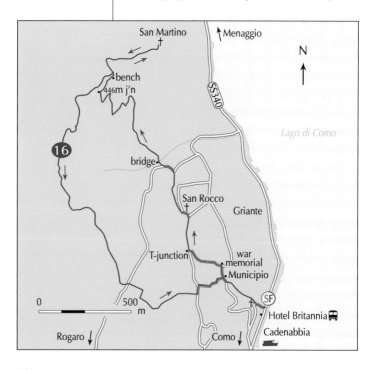

are breathtaking views over the lake. A shady picnic area invites walkers to enjoy the place.

Retrace your steps via the gully then fork immediately R before the **bench**. This lovely high path, with far-reaching views, narrows a little, passing a small house and bears SW with a stretch of handrail. At the next fork go L (for Griante) heading S. Soon you plunge down rocky flanks and past small properties. Steps with pebbles take you down to a stream – cross straight over (ignoring turn-offs) for a short climb to follow a fenced property. As you leave the woodland a lane takes over SE to the Rogaro–Griante road.

Cross onto Via Cima dei Ronchi over a rise and quickly downhill, veering R past gated properties. Some 80 metres on, don't miss the overgrown path L into the woodland. Surprise surprise! You find yourself on an old cobbled way winding E downhill. It merges into Via per Brughée, which is lined with villas and gardens. As you reach a road go L then next R on Via Franzani past an *Alimentari* (grocery store). Cross straight over Via Brentano (near the Municipio) onto stepped Via Mazzini, as per the ascent route. This leads back to **Cadenabbia** (201m, 1hr 15min) on the lakeside.

*San Martino perches high above the lake*

# WALK 17
*The Bocchetta di Nava Traverse*

| | |
|---|---|
| **Start** | Croce, Hotel Adler |
| **Finish** | Cadenabbia bus stop |
| **Distance** | 9km (5.6 miles) |
| **Ascent/Descent** | 500m/685m |
| **Difficulty** | Grade 2 |
| **Walking time** | 3hr 15min (+ 1hr 30min extension) |
| **Access** | From Menaggio take bus C12 for the short trip up to Croce; the bus stop is opposite Hotel Adler. A C10 bus (ASF) or ferry can be used for the return to Menaggio. |

A lovely walk up through woods and pasture beneath towering peaks. The return meanders downhill on an old military track across carpets of sun-drenched Mediterranean flora and is accompanied by simply magnificent lake views.

Towards the end, an optional and highly recommended detour can be made to the wonderful belvedere of San Martino (see Walk 16); either way the day concludes on the lovely waterfront at Cadenabbia, part of Griante. Drinking water and a picnic should be carried as there is nothing en route.

From the bus stop and **Hotel Adler** at **Croce** (392m) turn R along the road past the church, and follow signs for 'Golf', which entails forking L up Via A Wyatt. At the old wash trough fork R as per red/white waymarking for n.2, Via dei Monti Lariani. After a concrete-based lane, bear R onto a grass ramp and up across the road to a flight of steps. A delightful sunken way climbs for a while through shady deciduous woodland. At a minor road, go L uphill and around a corner to the immaculate, whitewashed chapel **Madonna delle Grazie di Paullo**.

Here turn L on the gravel lane, Via ai Monti di Nava, past houses scattered here and there in pretty woodland and fields. The way continues straight through **Miè**

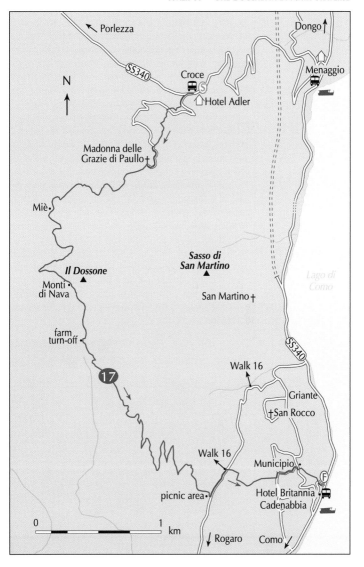

(685m), a cluster of modest buildings and a signpost at an intersection of lanes. Hazelnut and chestnut trees are common, succeeded by beech as you ascend. Marked regularly with red/white paint splashes, the lane veers SE in constant ascent, coming out at last near the meadows and summer houses of **Monti di Nava** (885m, 1hr 30min), overshadowed by massive Monte Crocione.

Stay on the lane as it heads S in gentle descent past a modest **farm** where an arrow points you L off the lane/n.2 and into the cover of woodland. Soon a series of tight zigzags indicate that this was once a military road, although it gives way to a rougher stony path bearing L (SE) across limestone mountain flanks with superb views over the lake and the peninsula with Bellagio. This is a simply beautiful descent route. Below is Griante, an assemblage of villas and gardens, while closer at hand to the north the precipitous outcrop of Sasso di San Martino, with its tiny landmark church, stands out. Back in woodland again, ignore a fork R for the Cappella degli Alpini, then keep L at the ensuing junction. This finally reaches rural properties then a picnic area with a drinking fountain next to a minor road from Rogaro (1hr 15min). Turn L and follow this road.

*Monti di Nava and the Crocione*

A few minutes along is the signed turn-off L for **San Martino** should you have the desire and energy to make the lovely detour – slot into Walk 16, allow an extra 1hr 30min and be prepared to follow the description in reverse.

*The church of San Martino is a worthwhile detour*

Opposite the San Martino turn-off, branch R onto Via Cima dei Ronchi over a rise and quickly downhill, veering R past gated properties. Some 80 metres on, don't miss the overgrown path L into the woodland. Surprise surprise! You find yourself on an old cobbled way winding E downhill. It merges into Via per Brughée, which is lined with villas and gardens. As you reach a road go L then next R on Via Franzani past an Alimentari (grocery store). Cross straight over Via Brentano (near the Municipio) onto a stepped way (Via Mazzini). This leads down to Via Roma and the main lakeside road in the vicinity of Hotel Britannia at lovely **Cadenabbia** (200m, 30min).

The ferry wharf is a short distance to the R, while the bus stop to return to Menaggio is immediately opposite.

# WALK 18
### Crocetta

| | |
|---|---|
| **Start/Finish** | Croce, Hotel Adler |
| **Distance** | 3.5km (2.2 miles) |
| **Ascent/Descent** | 110m/110m |
| **Difficulty** | Grade 1 |
| **Walking time** | 1hr |
| **Access** | From Menaggio take bus C12 for the short trip up to Croce; the bus stop is opposite Hotel Adler. **Note** It is possible to drive as far as the termination of Via GB Pigato, where you can park. |

It takes very little effort to get to the Crocetta, 'little cross', for a beautiful bird's-eye view over the township of Menaggio along with inspiring vistas up and down the lake. A further bonus is the chance to explore a web of trenches that snake through the trees high above the lake shore. Belonging to the Linea Cadorna, they date back to 1912–16 when Italy feared invasion (see Introduction).

This is an easy, short walk that begins on a quiet surfaced road and moves onto lanes in shady woodland, good for stretching your legs in preparation for longer outings.

From the bus stop at **Croce** (392m) turn R along the road past the church, and follow signs for 'Golf', which entails forking L up Via A Wyatt. You pass an old washing trough still gushing water. Ignore the path L where Walk 17 branches off. Even from here the lake views are lovely!

Not long after a hairpin bend in the road you fork L on Via GB Pigato. The last of the houses is soon passed and you enter the woodland on a shady lane. Nearby is a sign and the start of the shelters and **trench system** belonging to the Linea Cadorna – take some time out to explore.

*Gorgeous views over Menaggio and the northern lake*

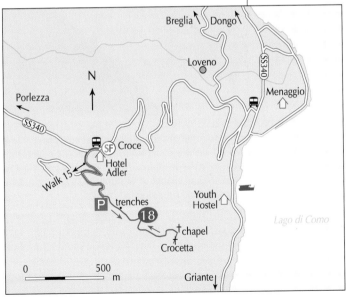

*A trench near Crocetta*

Close at hand is Monte Grona (north), while to the northeast the light grey peaks of the Lepontine rise at the head of the lake. The rugged Grigne stand out due east.

Then resume the lane for a short uphill stretch to a fenced clearing with chestnut trees and a hut. Branch L here to find more historic trenches and then the Capella degli Alpini **chapel** in a stunning spot overlooking Menaggio and Lago di Como. ◄

Near the chapel an arrow on a tree points through the wood SSW on a clear path to where the wooden cross **Crocetta** (40min, 502m) stands on the breathtaking edge of a cliff. The view from here is dominated by the Bellagio promontory and the lovely Lecco branch of the lake.

Retrace your steps back to the bus stop at **Croce** (392m, 20min).

# WALK 19

*Val Sanagra*

| | |
|---|---|
| **Start/Finish** | Menaggio, Piazza Garibaldi |
| **Distance** | 14km (8.7 miles) |
| **Ascent/Descent** | 550m/550m |
| **Difficulty** | Grade 2 |
| **Walking time** | 5hr 20min |
| **Access** | Menaggio has excellent ferry and bus links. The walk start is located close to the lakefront, in the pedestrian-only zone. Local Menaggio buses serve Naggio and Codogna on the return. **Note** It is possible to drive as far as Piamuro, where there is a small car park. |

A wonderful long and varied outing, experiencing old cobbled mule tracks, scattered mountain hamlets and summer pastures, a dramatic cascading river, water-powered mills, pretty villages and woodland, as well as elegant villas and charming homes in Menaggio and nearby Loveno, where, from the late 1800s, patrician families would spend their vacations.

After climbing up from the lakeside through quiet residential areas dotted with stately villas, the walk enters the Val Sanagra. Good, signed paths cross ravines on stone bridges to reach summer pastures and long-established hamlets. Note that the paths in the uppermost valley are little frequented and can be a little overgrown (check at the Menaggio Tourist Office if in doubt). The return follows the west side of the valley, taking in pretty villages – Naggio is outstanding – with some stretches on quiet farm roads. Take a picnic unless you plan on lunching at the Mulino Chioderia (tel 0344 041791).

From waterfront Piazza Garibaldi at **Menaggio** (202m) take pedestrian Via Calvi up to the main road; duck L then immediately R around the church and proceed along Via Caronti. Turn R up pedestrianised Via Leoni and soon L on cobbled Via Castellino da Castello, which incorporates the remains of medieval castle walls. Lovingly

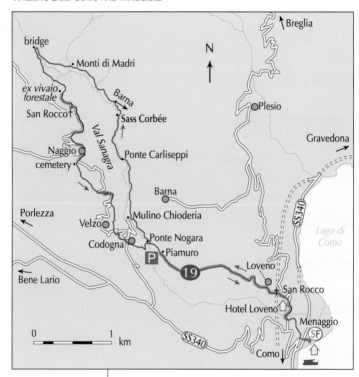

tended gardens and pretty villas punctuate the uphill stretch, along with inspiring lake views. When you reach the road for Plesio, turn R across the modest Sanagra river to **Hotel Loveno** and a bus stop, where you fork L up a flight of steps.

Another short stretch of road will see you at the shrine to **San Rocco**; go L past a clutch of signposts and into quiet **Loveno**. Through Piazza Milius veer R uphill past old residences and beautiful villas. At a war memorial go L to follow the road, skirting the parkland of Hotel Royal and past the baroque façade of San Lorenzo church near Villa Vigoni. Now yellow/black signs point you L rather steeply up the tarmac way, to conclude the surfaced section at a cemetery and car park at **Piamuro** (374m, 50min), as well as the entrance to the Parco della Val Sanagra.

Branch L (NNW) on the lane marked n.4 across a flat meadow edged with woodland at the foot of Monte Grona. This bears NW through farmland and over a rise with a shrine. It's not far downhill to the first of a series of photogenic bridges, **Ponte Nogara** (393m) over the Sanagra. However, the path keeps to the pretty right bank, past a tinkling cascade and a stretch of stream popular with dippers. Not far along, after an old furnace,

*Bridge near Mulino Chioderia*

is another lovely bridge close to the **Mulino Chioderia** (412m, 30min), once a mill and water-powered nail factory, now a trout farm and country-style restaurant. Keep R on the lane past the fish troughs and into the narrowing river valley. Derelict mills dot the peaceful, shady way. Ignore the forks for Barna, and continue to a tiny hamlet and mill and elegant stone bridge – **Ponte Carliseppi** (456m) – where you cross to the L bank.

The path on the ensuing stretch is a little rough and follows close to the river, which is wilder here. At a dramatic ravine with lovely pools and a massive limestone overhang, a footbridge crosses to the R bank. The path, narrow but clear and marked red/white, soon reaches a huge boulder apparently blocking the valley. This is **Sass Corbée**. Steps cut into the rock – aided by a handrail – lead upwards. The red/white-marked path weaves its way in and out of fallen rocks, gradually gaining height in woodland dotted with gorgeous cyclamens. The going is cool and shady, and may be slippery.

Not far up, a wider path (from Barna) is joined at an old limekiln, Forno della Calce. Go L (NW) here as the going levels out between old drystone walls, high above the river. Several clearings and minor side streams are traversed and huddles of simple houses, long abandoned, bear witness to the erstwhile settlements and life in Val Sanagra. The path is occasionally messy where the stream has overflowed, finally emerging on to a lovely peaceful pasture subject to the inexorable invasion of brambles. This is **Monti di Madri** (570m, 1hr 15min).

A faint path follows the watercourse upstream for about 10min to a timber **bridge** (640m) which you cross. On the opposite bank a narrow but clear path veers L past another small limekiln and joins a wider rough track. This climbs steadily SW to a field and the **ex vivaio forestale** (former forestry nursery, 701m). The track is now surfaced and continues through dense woodland with the occasional glimpse to Monte Grona (northwest), not to mention the wild valley below. At the chapel of **San Rocco** (761m, drinking water) turn L on a quiet road. Not far down, fork L on a lovely stepped way, then resume the road to a second shortcut which leads straight into the cool alleyways and tiny squares of the charming old village of **Naggio** (657m, 1hr).

Down in Piazza San Antonio walk past the front of the eponymous church and bus stop, ignoring the road sign for Menaggio, and through to the **cemetery**. Here is a sign for the 'Strada Vecchia per Codogna' (the old road for Codogna), a shady grassy lane that heads S. Further on, it shares a couple of bends with the road, then (where a path forks L for Vecchia Chioderia – ignore) the mule track resumes S through fields, with the bonus of lake views. The actual village of Velzo is bypassed, and you cross the road once more in the vicinity of a huge church. The magnificent Grigne mountains rise ahead, beyond Lago di Como. The track drops to nearby **Codogna** (450m) and elegant Villa Camozzi. Only metres below is the start of a delightful cobbled way signed for **Piamuro**. Once through the houses, it winds its way down to **Ponte Nogara** (393m, 1hr) encountered on the outward route.

Now retrace your steps back to **Piamuro** (15min), then on to **Loveno** and **Menaggio** (220m, 40min).

*Ponte Nogara*

# WALK 20

## Rifugio Menaggio and Monte Grona

| | |
|---|---|
| **Start/Finish** | Breglia |
| **Distance** | 9km (5.6 miles) |
| **Ascent/Descent** | 950m/950m |
| **Difficulty** | Grade 2+ |
| **Walking time** | 4hr 40min (+ 1hr/1hr 30min extensions) |
| **Access** | From Menaggio take bus C13 to Breglia. By car, drive up the winding road to the village, then proceed on narrow Via ai Monti di Breglia to the parking area at Monti di Breglia, saving 1hr 40min. A modest toll is charged for this last stretch. |
| **Note** | A Sept 2022 landslip led to the temporary closure of the path between Rifugio Menaggio and La Forcoletta. See the rifugio website for updates. |

This absolutely superb walk on the steep mountainous flanks of Monte Grona, to the rear of the lakeside village of Menaggio, makes a memorable day out. Clear paths traverse pasture, woodland and open grassland to an elongated crest with spectacular views to the spread of the Alps as well as over beautiful Lago di Como. Lengthy uphill sections are tackled in the outgoing section, so go prepared and fit. A hospitable mountain refuge, Rifugio Menaggio, is visited, handy for lunch or refreshments, or an overnight stay.

One extension leads to the summit of Monte Grona: note that this is rather narrow and tricky in spots, so a head for heights and sure footedness are essential (Grade 3). A second easier extension climbs to the Bregagnino.

The laid-back rural village of Breglia (see Walk 21), perched dizzily above the lake, has a handy hotel and café/restaurant – Albergo Breglia – close to the bus stop.

◄ From the bus stop opposite the cemetery at **Breglia** (748m) turn L up Via ai Monti di Breglia, heading mostly N. A short distance uphill, after a water trough on a corner, fork R for the path marked red/white that avoids the tarmac. It shortcuts through woodland, crosses the road and continues uphill past a house. When it emerges on the road near a cableway, turn R for a short stretch, then after a watercourse the path resumes uphill via houses and meadows.

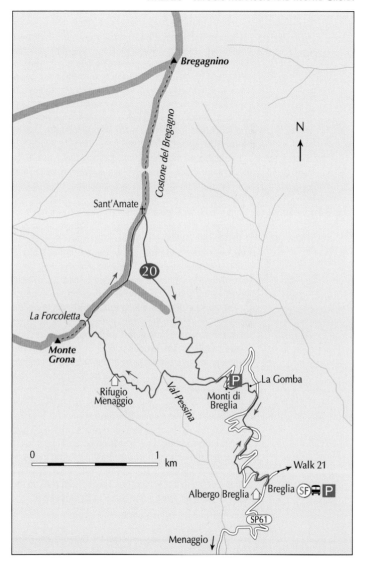

After a further road crossing, a steep and possibly muddy path leads through old chestnut terraces past ruined stone houses. **Note** A short way up, ignore arrows pointing R, and keep straight ahead. Lined with bushes of fragrant broom, the way soon rejoins the road, bearing R to a fountain and picnic tables with great views. A signed path now points you L to a concrete/stone ramp past **La Gomba**. Steps through a woodland of silver birch and ferns lead to a picnic table and the parking area at **Monti di Breglia** (1085m, 1hr).

A matter of minutes uphill, the way forks: turn L for the Sentiero Basso, initially W along a lane. Approaching Val Pessina this narrows, soon beginning a steep zigzag climb into hazel woodland. ◄

The cableway for the refuge ahead runs overhead, though lengths of cable occasionally lie across the path – watch your step.

It will be with great satisfaction that you emerge from the cover of trees to the clearing with **Rifugio Menaggio** (1383m, 1hr) and its drinking fountain (open mid-June to mid-September and most weekends, tel 0344 1930017 www.rifugiomenaggio.eu). The refuge has stunning views towards Lecco and the rugged Grigne to the east, without forgetting the lake. Refreshments and meals are on offer.

At the rear of the building fork uphill, following the signs for Monte Grona 'via normale'. Wasting no time, the clear if narrow path gains height over stony ground to the saddle of **La Forcoletta** (1627m, 45min), in the company of huge black crows and swallows. For Monte Grona take the following route, but be aware that it rates Grade 3 on difficulty.

### Extension to Monte Grona (1hr return)

Turn L (SW) up a shoulder that quickly becomes steep and exposed, demanding some hands-on scrambling. It leads gradually below the main ridge, finally gaining the summit of **Monte Grona** (1730m, 30min) with amazing views that even take in the Matterhorn. Take special care on the steep descent on loose stones back to **La Forcoletta**.

---

Turn R (NE) on the clear path along the broad grassy crest, Costone del Bregagno. A thrilling glimpse of glaciated

Monte Rosa to the west is enjoyed, along with a sweep of the lake beyond Bellagio and down as far as Lecco. The grey Grigne stand out to the east, while at the head of the lake are the Lepontine Alps with Monte Disgrazia. The undulating pasture has colourful patches of purple-blue gentians, heather and pretty pink alpenrose. The next landmark, the modest chapel of **Sant'Amate** (1617m, 15min), also offers a beautiful outlook northwest to Lago di Lugano. For even vaster views, consider the following extension, a straightforward route up a broad crest.

*A scenic pause during the ascent to Monte Grona*

### Extension to Breganino (1hr 30min return)

In common with the VML route – Via dei Monti Lariani – take the well-worn path marked in red/white for the steady 300m ascent due N. Pauses to get your breath back will come in useful to enjoy the ever-improving views. The **Bregagnino** (1902m, 1hr) is a lookout *par excellence* over the upper lake and the vast spread of the Lepontine Alps, with ice and snow-capped peaks galore. Return to **Sant'Amate** (1617m, 30min) the way you came.

*The broad grassy crest leading to Sant'Amate*

For the descent, take the signed path SSE, a diagonal traverse of a spectacular mountainside with dizzying lake views. It drops past a radio mast where Rifugio Menaggio can be seen. Down in woodland once more, ignore turn-offs and finally pass the Sentiero Basso fork, before reaching **Monti di Breglia** again (1085m, 1hr 10min).

Unless you're lucky enough to bag a lift, the rest of the descent to **Breglia** (748m, 40min) is the same as the outward route.

# WALK 21

*San Domenico and the Santuario di Breglia*

| | |
|---|---|
| **Start/Finish** | Breglia |
| **Distance** | 3km (1.8 miles) |
| **Ascent/Descent** | 60m/60m |
| **Difficulty** | Grade 1 |
| **Walking time** | 1hr 15min |
| **Access** | Bus C13 from Menaggio goes to Breglia; it is feasible to drive up and there's a spacious car park at the village entrance. |

High above Menaggio and the lake, this is a pleasant, easy stroll through beautiful chestnut woodland. It circles the 865m Motto outcrop, chosen by local inhabitants for both a sanctuary and a tiny shrine on the dizzying cliff edge, with expansive views across Lago di Como. The sanctuary dates back to 1781, and houses a revered statue of the Madonna sculpted in marble.

The tranquil village of Breglia is located on a broad saddle well below the forbidding ridge of Monte Grona-Bregagnino, and has a friendly café-hotel-restaurant near the walk start.

Breglia has been a place of transit for centuries. There is a Roman tomb (6th century AD) opposite the bus stop; tombs were placed at the roadside to keep the memory of the dead alive, and a road ran through Breglia en route to a trans-alpine crossing. The village name derives from the Celtic for 'bridge' or 'passage'.

From the bus stop at **Breglia** (748m) walk across to the car park. In the far R corner take the lane that leads into woodland, and keep L at the fork soon encountered. Initially on a level, it starts a gentle climb SE past some beautiful aged chestnut trees and remnants of man-made terraces from the times when chestnuts were part of the staple diet locally.

En route through gaps in the foliage you are tempted with sparkling views of the vast lake below, but

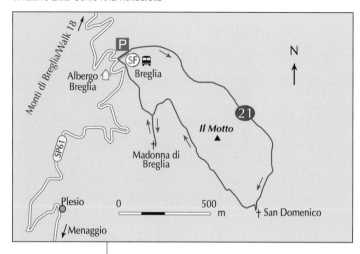

*The Santuario della Madonna di Breglia*

you have to wait until the tiny chapel of **San Domenico** (800m) for the breathtaking ones, undeniably worth waiting for! But do watch your step on the rocks here.

The lane continues NW around the mountain. At a pasture clearing turn L and soon go L again to join the broad cobbled stepped way (aka Via Crucis) lined with the mini shrines of the stations of the cross. On a prominent outcrop, the white church known as the **Santuario della Madonna di Breglia** (770m) offers yet more wonderful views.

Once you've had your fill of panoramas, go back down the stepped way and keep straight on. This will bring you down to houses, concluding at the bus stop at **Breglia** (748m, 1hr 15min).

# WALK 22

*Gravedona to Domaso*

| | |
|---|---|
| **Start** | Gravedona ferry wharf |
| **Finish** | Domaso ferry wharf |
| **Distance** | 4km (2.5 miles) |
| **Ascent/Descent** | 200m/200m |
| **Difficulty** | Grade 1–2 |
| **Walking time** | 1hr 30min |
| **Access** | Gravedona and Domaso are served by hydrofoil and ferry services and bus line C10. |

This appealing walk wanders through quiet hamlets and vineyards high above the northwestern shore of the lake, well away from crowds. The paths and lanes have waymarking. Be aware of the presence of steep flights of steps – worthy of the vertical Amalfi Coast! A longish stretch of surfaced road is followed on the middle section, but it is used only by locals.

Domaso is a lovely spot for lunch at a lakeside café or restaurant. Its historic heart, with narrow alleyways and elegant buildings, also merits a visit.

Don't miss the graceful chequered black-and-white 12th-century Romanesque Chiesa di Santa Maria del Tiglio, on the waterfront, a short stroll south from Gravedona ferry wharf, past the Tourist Office. Another point of interest is the home of the great scientist Alessandro Volta (of electrical fame), native of Gravedona, passed early in the walk.

▶ From the ferry wharf at **Gravedona** (201m) go R (N) along the waterfront to **Piazza Mazzini**. Turn L here (at a sign for Ristorante Ca' de' Matt) through to Via al Castello where you go R then L up Via G Dentore. This leads through a square, where you continue on Via San Rocco to the main road.

The route can be linked with Walk 23 from Domaso to Gera Lario.

Turn R past the **Municipio** and a sign for Volta's house, and soon L up the alley Via Dossi e Segna, soon forking R for Via Pessina. A lovely way, it passes beneath

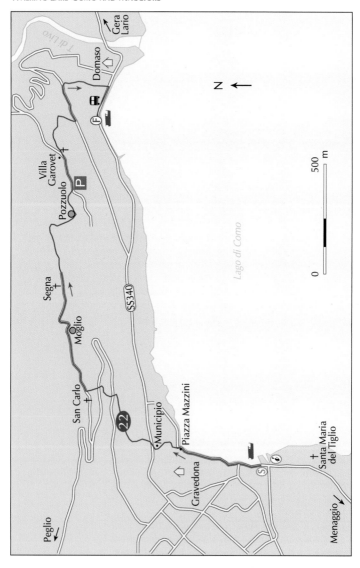

a road and proceeds quite steeply up to a fork at a house with huge gates. Go L to the road and continue straight up past houses. This concludes in the vicinity of the **Chiesa di San Carlo** (350m, 30min), where swallows make good use of the tower.

Turn R (E) on the narrow surfaced road to enjoy great views over the northern curve of the lake and wooded promontories. Below is the Gravedona power station. After the houses of **Moglio** comes the final climb, to the rural settlement of **Segna** (395m), complete with a tiny church, San Lorenzo. Walk through to the last of the modest houses and a wash trough, where the road reverts to a lane, passing well-kept vegetable gardens. The unusual outlook from here takes in the mouth of the Adda river, where it empties into Lago di Como at Colico – the different coloured waters of river and lake provide a dramatic contrast.

A short way along (about 100m) fork R (E) off the lane on a small path between stone walls. This makes its way diagonally downhill through vineyards and cultivated terraces flanked by woodland and into the

*Houses set high above the lake*

*Old drinking fountain
at Pozzuolo*

charming hamlet of **Pozzuolo** (310m). Among its delightful features are a cool fountain and trough used by the locals to chill their drinks.

*It's worth making a short detour right to the church and benches for enjoying lake views.*

◀ Down at Piazza Acone and a car park, follow the tarmac the short distance to a shrine opposite **Villa Garovet** and branch R onto a lovely stepped lane. Leading downhill it reaches houses. Where the steps end, keep L on a pedestrian way across a stream on a level, then R down to Piazza Feloy Leonardo and a car park. Now follow the sign for Ristorante La Contrada through a district distinguished by elegant houses.

You emerge on the main road and waterfront of **Domaso** (201m), where benches shaded by Stone Pine trees overlook a pebble beach with a view back to Gravedona and its landmark church. Inviting cafés and eateries are dotted along the waterfront. Turn R for the ferry wharf or the bus stop.

# WALK 23

*Domaso to Gera Lario*

| | |
|---|---|
| **Start** | Domaso ferry wharf |
| **Finish** | Gera Lario bus stop |
| **Distance** | 7.5km (4.6 miles) |
| **Ascent/Descent** | 280m/280m |
| **Difficulty** | Grade 2 |
| **Walking time** | 2hr 20min |
| **Access** | Domaso is served by hydrofoil and ferry services and bus line C10. From Gera Lario take the C10 bus as no ferries call in. |

Located on the quiet top northwestern shore of Lago di Como, Domaso has a charming historic centre. From the lakefront the route climbs through woodland to a succession of photogenic villages of age-old stone houses and narrow alleyways; Aurogna is particularly attractive. En route are wonderful sweeping views of the northern corner of Lago di Como, its water dyed different hues of blue and milky grey by the Adda and Mera rivers that empty their load of glacial debris and earth into the lake. Gera Lario is a very popular spot for windsurfers thanks to the strong breezes that prevail at the top of the lake.

▶ From the ferry wharf at **Domaso** (201m) walk along the lakeside promenade in the direction of Colico, as far as the bus stop at Piazza Ghislanzoni Oreste and its cafés. Fork diagonally R along the alleyway, Via Regina. This leads via an arched passageway through to Piazza Feloy and onto the imposing 18th-century **Chiesa di San Bartolomeo**. Walk past the entrance and take the road signed for Gaggio/Pozzolo, although you soon leave it for a narrow way across a stone bridge over the River Livo. A stepped cobbled way now leads upwards to a chapel dedicated to San Silvestro, where you keep L, passing houses and pretty gardens. There are lovely views over to Colico and the mouth of the River Adda.

This route is a logical continuation of Walk 22 between Gravedona and Domaso.

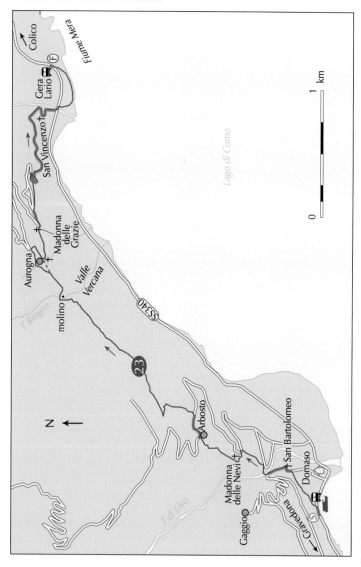

At the road, take the path signed for **Madonna delle Nevi**, not far off. The church was erected in the 1600s in memory of victims of a plague that swept the district. Here the path enters a short rock tunnel bored into the mountainside, then climbs to a road where the restored stepped track branches R. Further up this goes R to cross a stream, ascending to **Arbosto** (354m, 45min) with its war memorial, square and Chiesa di San Salvatore.

Turn R along the road past Ristorante Bellavista. After a café-tobacconist, ignore Via Arbosto then branch L up a cobbled lane that heads uphill past orchards. After crossing a road it enters woodland interspersed with fields, climbing steadily and flanked by stone walls and patches of nettles. Ignore the fork near a shrine. At a road near modern terraced apartments, turn R to where a lane coasts through woodland and passes a picnic table. A gentle ascent NE touches on pasture and abandoned stone houses, along with excellent views to the Mera and Adda rivers with their backdrop of the light grey peaks of the Alps edging on Valtellina. Through flourishing chestnut woodland the way narrows to a path and drops into Valle Vercana, past a tiny stone **molino** (mill).

*Approaching
Valle Vercana*

*Old stone houses in Aurogna*

After crossing the cascading Brugna torrent, the path emerges into cultivated fields and widens. As the lane begins to descend towards asphalt and power lines, branch L onto a path past an old building and through well-kept vegetable gardens (or see the shortcut below). A footbridge across a stream leads straight into the beautiful old hamlet of **Aurogna** (420m, 45min). Continue in the same direction past the Municipio. Not far on, at a building featuring a modest Madonna fresco (house n.7), turn sharp R downhill out of the village to meet tarmac, and R again to a new flight of steps down to a shrine.

**Shortcut to bypass Aurogna**

If for some reason you're in a hurry, instead of branching L towards the village, stick to the lane as it crosses a stream and fork immediately R on new steps to the shrine and the main route.

---

Veer L across the meadow to where the old way and stone wall resumes through mixed woodland, as well as plenty of walnut trees and grape vines. Soon after the **Chiesa di Madonna delle Grazie** comes a short stretch of tarmac (SP2). It's not far to a junction where you keep L to drop under the road for a path past houses. The road is joined again briefly to the solemn grey **Chiesa di San Vincenzo** that dates back to the 1400s.

Cross over the main road and go L across the river to take the cycleway down to the lovely lakeside, complete with a marina and hub for windsurfers. At the car park and café, turn L for the main road and bus stop in **Gera Lario** (200m, 50min).

*The imposing Chiesa di San Vincenzo*

# WALK 24
## *Around Bellagio*

| | |
|---|---|
| **Start/Finish** | Bellagio ferry piers |
| **Distance** | 6km (3.7 miles) |
| **Ascent/Descent** | 85m/85m |
| **Difficulty** | Grade 1 |
| **Walking time** | 2hr |
| **Access** | Frequent ferries visit Bellagio from ports on the western shore of Lago di Como, as well as the car ferry from Varenna on the eastern bank; it can also be reached by bus from Como and Lecco |

An easy stroll around the beautiful surrounds of the lakeside town of Bellagio, justifiably renowned for its spectacular location on a dramatic mountainous promontory in the middle of the lake. Old paved ways pass through perfectly terraced gardens, olive groves, fishing hamlets and stately villas set in vast parkland. The walk is a good introduction to this central part of Lago di Como as villages on both sides of the headland are visited, and you can see across the water to where rugged ridges dwarf far-off settlements.

While the route appears initially rather short, it will mysteriously stretch out to occupy at least half a day as myriad detours beckon, or even longer if you stop off at the gardens of Villa Melzi, not to mention take time out for a leisurely lunch – restaurants are to be found at Pescallo, San Giovanni and Loppia.

From the lakefront and ferry piers at **Bellagio** (202m), opposite the Tourist Office start up the stepped alley Salita Mella between boutiques and restaurants. At the top is bustling Via Garibaldi. It's worth making the brief detour L to the square hosting the main church; in the top R corner is a photogenic medieval watchtower.

Resume Via Garibaldi L (S) past shops and restaurants to where the Municipio stands alongside the tiny

*Salita Mella at the beginning of the walk*

11th-century Chiesa di San Giorgio – you need the stepped alley opposite, L. It's a gentle uphill at first, between walled gardens before heading downhill towards the water. You branch R on Via Sfondrati past pretty flower-decked houses to the peaceful waterfront of **Pescallo** (199m). As the name suggests, it was once an important fishing village, with its own market. Relax on a bench to drink in the panorama taking in the Lecco arm of the lake backed by the light grey Grigne range of mountains. Nearby is Piazza del Porto with Hotel/Ristorante La Pergola. Take the road, Via Pescallo, gently uphill to the **cemetery** on the right-hand corner where many foreign residents have been laid to rest.

Here, at the crossroads, turn L on the pavement of Via Valassina alongside long-established olive groves which give this district its name: Oliveiro. Past a road junction for Bellagio, soon historic greenhouses mark the start of the remarkable property of **Villa Giulia**.

Originally dating back to 1624, **Villa Giulia** was completely overhauled and redesigned in the late

1700s by Count Pietro Venini and renamed to honour his wife. He had a huge swathe of land flattened in front of the building and fashioned into a broad avenue so as to grace the villa with access and views to both branches of the lake.

Turn R now onto this curious '**Vialone**'-cum-vast meadow with an amazing outlook west to the Crocione crest high over Griante. Don't go all the way to the far end, but fork L on the first minor road you reach. Not far up cross over for the cobbled way (Via Taronico) straight ahead past houses. This curves right to become a stepped path, gently progressing uphill with impressive views

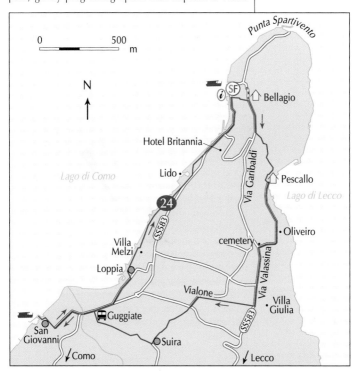

back northwest to Monte Grona and Menaggio standing out against a backdrop of the upper lake.

The tiny square of **Suira** (282m) is reached, surrounded by elegant dwellings. Turn R here for the pedestrian alley Via Monumento, flanked by high walls and gardens. A short way downhill, keep L on Via La Derta, a lovely if steepish descent comprising 266 daunting steps to an old villa and Piazza Sant'Andrea at **Guggiate** (209m).

A café and bus stop are located on the main road where you turn L with care. Not far along, after a river crossing, fork R onto a quiet road amid parkland into charming **San Giovanni** (203m), with its fascinating museum of instruments for navigation (tel 031 950309 www.bellagiomuseo.com). Turn R down Via Pescatori to the lakeside and ferry wharf, directly opposite Villa Carlotta and the spread of Cadenabbia on the opposite shore.

Retrace your steps to **Guggiate** and continue on for a matter of minutes before forking L down to the tiny waterfront hamlet of **Loppia** (197m), once home to fishermen. It is here that the tree-lined Vialone concludes with steps down to an ornamental gate. On the waterside, don't miss the elegant traditional lake rowing boats and massive old barges used until the late 1900s for transporting goods and livestock. After a restaurant is the entrance to **Villa Melzi**, well worth the modest entrance fee for the relaxing lakefront pathway and a wander around the spectacular beds of rhododendrons and camellias in the beautiful English-style garden (www.giardinidivillamelzi. it). Otherwise, detour the gardens via the road, watching out for traffic.

The two routes join up at the far end of the Melzi property, passing the once-grand **Lido** to the lakefront promenade where flourishing flowerbeds and a blaze of giant oleanders are interspersed with benches, perfect for drinking in the glorious uplake panorama in the company of ducks and cormorants. Past the monumental old **Hotel Britannia**, long empty, you arrive back at the ferry piers of **Bellagio**.

# WALK 25

*Belvedere del Monte Nuvolone*

| | |
|---|---|
| **Start** | Guggiate bus stop |
| **Finish** | Ristorante La Baita bus stop, Parco San Primo |
| **Distance** | 14km (8.7 miles) |
| **Ascent/Descent** | 1130m/240m |
| **Difficulty** | Grade 2 |
| **Walking time** | 4hr 15min |
| **Access** | Guggiate is a short bus trip south from Bellagio on the C30 line; the C36 bus serves Parco San Primo throughout the summer months – check the timetable for return runs. Both are managed by ASF. |

This is a protracted climb on old paved mule tracks and good paths to a wonderful belvedere over Lago di Como. The mountain's name is a reference to 'large cloud', but try and time your visit for a clear day, for instance immediately after stormy weather, when the views north will stretch all the way to the snow-capped Alps. En route are many great viewpoints, but all are eclipsed by the breathtaking panorama that awaits at the top. The Belvedere del Nuvolone is not the actual peak, as this is shrouded in trees, but a perch on the northernmost extremity of a thickly wooded ridge high over Bellagio. It is simply superb.

Afterwards, saturated with vastness, walkers can either retrace their steps to Guggiate or proceed to the Monte San Primo Park and catch the bus back (or take a taxi).

▶ From the bus stop at **Guggiate** (202m) cross the cobbled square (Piazza Sant'Andrea) and turn sharp R on Via Ciceri, flanking a villa. After a stream crossing you start up a stepped path S, winding up to houses and a road. Following signs for the 'Dorsale Lariano' (the Lariano ridge route), take the quiet surfaced road uphill through a rural area. Veering L it steepens and narrows between

Fit walkers can extend this route to include the spectacular higher summit ridge of Monte San Primo – see Walk 26.

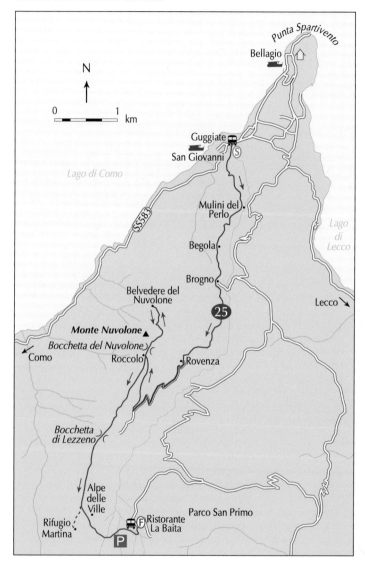

stone walls up to modest farms with lovely lake views (Cognanica, 304m).

Still essentially S, a lane takes over, coming out at **Mulini del Perlo** (360m, 30min), where you will find old mills on a stream. An atmospheric sunken path proceeds upwards, shaded by chestnut trees on the climb to **Begola**. Here the way widens to a level lane and leads to an old property with iron railings and the scatter of houses that go under the name of **Brogno** (605m, 45min), although you'll be hard put to find a sign to that effect. The road resumes here, but you leave it soon – take care not to miss the turn R at a bridge for path n.1. Ignore the road ahead signed for Belvedere.

The narrow road S soon becomes a concrete ramp then a path through hazel woodland. A clearing with a shrine allows inspiring views south to the Monte San Primo crest. A lane now leads through the houses of **Rovenza** (723m, 30min), where there is drinking water and a magnificent view of the main pyramidal Grigna peak to the east.

Still on n.1, turn R up the quiet road past farms and face 30min/200m in ascent to where a dirt lane forks R (NNE) – the relevant sign for 'Belvedere del Nuvolone' may be partly concealed by foliage. The clear way narrows to a path through woodland. Keep L at a fork in gentle ascent past several modest houses. You emerge in the clearing of the **Roccolo** (934m), an old stone hunter's hut surrounded by rowan trees hung with cages to attract birds. There are plunging views west down to the Como branch of the lake.

Nearby is the saddle **Bocchetta del Nuvolone**, where the path skirts to the R (N) around the edge of Monte Nuvolone, and heads up a brief scrambly passage. After more huts in silver birch and conifers, fork R soon for the final 5min onto the dizzy **Belvedere del Nuvolone** (1025m, 1hr). Almost at your feet is Bellagio on its lake promontory, while north is the spread of the Alps, and northeast the pyramid of Monte Legnone.

Return to **Roccolo** (934m, 30min) and either retrace your steps to **Guggiate**, allowing around 2hr 30min, or

*From the Belvedere del Nuvolone, the great Grigna stands out to the east*

take the 'Dorsale' (crest) path into the Parco San Primo, as follows.

Red/white waymarks point S through woodland with lake glimpses. At a house it widens to a lane, resuming as a level path further along. Continue through the saddle **Bocchetta di Lezzeno** (1006m) and up to a clearing with a huddle of huts and brilliant views to the Grigne, not to mention Monte San Primo, close at hand. A steady climb through beech woodland follows a barbed wire fence all the way to a meadow and pond (1182m, 1hr). Unless you still have the energy and desire for the final short 10min climb to 1221m **Rifugio Martina** – where more superb views along with delicious home-cooked meals are on offer (see Walk 26) – fork L here. An unsurfaced lane descends SE past **Alpe delle Ville** then E through beautiful beech woods. After the car park continue on to **Ristorante La Baita** and the bus stop (1100m, 30min).

# WALK 26

*Monte San Primo*

---

| | |
|---|---|
| **Start/Finish** | Ristorante La Baita bus stop, Parco San Primo |
| **Distance** | 7.5km (4.6 miles) |
| **Ascent/Descent** | 580m/580m |
| **Difficulty** | Grade 2+ |
| **Walking time** | 3hr 20min |
| **Access** | The ASF C36 bus links Bellagio with Parco San Primo throughout the summer months; otherwise drive to the walk start and park near Ristorante La Baita |

Thanks to the bus service, walkers can begin this must-do route to the 1682m summit of Monte San Primo at the 1100m mark, a great advantage. This memorable circuit takes you to the windswept ridge culminating in Monte San Primo, the highest point on the Triangolo Lariano. Thanks to its isolated position, towering over the Bellagio promontory, its brilliant panorama is truly something to write home about! It goes without saying that clear weather will optimise the experience.

Be aware that the route follows an extended steep and narrow path in ascent, which can get very slippery; the ridge and descent route are wider and more straightforward. Take a picnic unless you plan on eating at the popular family-run Rifugio Martina (tel 031 964695) encountered rather close to the start! There's always Ristorante La Baita at the end, although that means a meal without the view.

From the bus stop (1100m) near **Ristorante La Baita** in Parco San Primo, turn R on the unsurfaced lane signed for Rifugio Martina. Heading through magnificent beech woodland it swings W over a stream and past a derelict children's summer holiday home. Once through the car park and a gate, keep uphill past **Alpe delle Ville** to open pasture, then **Rifugio Martina** (1221m, 30min). This inviting eatery occupies a brilliant position with vast views up Lago di Como to the mountains beyond.

*Wonderful views from Rifugio Martina*

At the rear of the building a lane continues uphill to a clear signed path across meadows to follow the edge of beech woodland mixed with bracken. The going is already pretty steep, and loose stones and clay underfoot can make it slippery, so take your time. Pretty willow gentians and green alder shrubs brighten the way. You finally puff your way up to the crest; the summit of **Monte San Primo** and a cross (1682m, 1hr 15min) is a short climb to the L. The breathtaking views stretch towards the Po Plain and Milan, and well beyond the promontory of Bellagio up the lake to the Alps. On a fine day, you can see all the way northwest to the Matterhorn and Monte Rosa. The eastern flank of the lake features the rugged Grigne.

The mountain's namesake, **San Primo**, was a third-century Christian martyr who was condemned to death and put in a pit with bears; but – so the story goes – the creatures turned docile and lay down at his feet. A church in his name once stood on the mountaintop and devout Bellagians would climb up to light lamps there, but no trace remains of the building now.

The descent route takes the clear path ESE down the crest, keeping R around a knoll and crossing vast grassy slopes dotted with green alder, carline thistles and raspberries. Well below is the broad saddle of Pian del Tivano, famous for its limestone caves. Inspiring views range to the city of Lecco overshadowed by the Resegone. The broad saddle of **Bocchetta Terrabiotta** (1428m, 35min) is reached.

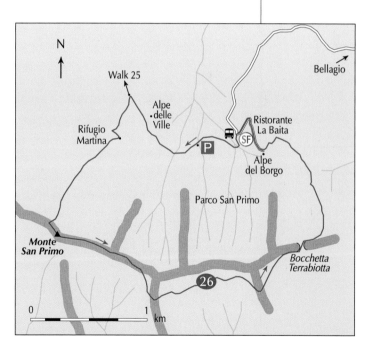

Cross the crest L (N) to the signpost for path n.1 (although you'll undoubtedly pause here to admire the amazing panorama down to Bellagio once more, as well as the orange roofs of Alpe del Borgo below). The path now curves towards N below Monte Ponciv, punctuated with aerials. In constant descent, you follow the edge of beautiful beech woodland, and veer W to the pasture clearings of the summer farm **Alpe del Borgo** (1170m). Here a narrow surfaced road leads past defunct ski lifts and down to the road with a car park, **Ristorante La Baita** and the bus stop (1100m, 1hr) where it all began.

# WALK 27

*The Strada Regia from Pognana Lario to Torno*

| | |
|---|---|
| **Start** | Pognana Lario ferry wharf |
| **Finish** | Torno ferry wharf |
| **Distance** | 10.5km (6.5 miles) |
| **Ascent/Descent** | 360m/360m |
| **Difficulty** | Grade 1–2 |
| **Walking time** | 3hr 30min (+ 20min extra side trip) |
| **Access** | Ferries on the Como–Bellagio run stop at Pognana Lario and Torno, as do buses on the C30 line |

The ferry stop at Pognana Lario is a tiny landing stage in a quiet cove, an especially pretty spot to start this highly recommended route. Medieval alleys and fascinating hidden corners of laid-back lakeside villages are explored, their cosy stone dwellings linked by tunnel-like cobbled passageways. It's worth allowing extra time to explore these hamlets; there's usually someone around, looking out of a window high above, to point you in the right direction should you lose your way in the maze of streets. Mules, used for transporting goods, can still be found labouring along the way, although most have been replaced by chugging miniature mechanical carriers and tractors.

Friendly local restaurants at Lemna and Molina can provide lunch or a picnic.

This walk follows in the footsteps of travellers on the **Strada Regia**, the 'royal road', in use from the 1600s to the early 1900s between Como and Bellagio on the northern tip of the Lario peninsula.

▶ From the ferry wharf at **Pognana Lario** (205m) take the abrupt flight of steps that will see you puffing up to the SS583 main road and bus stop. Cross straight over for stepped Via Canzaga which leads past old houses. Turn R up Via Sant'-Antonio, then next L through a delightful linked sequence of alleys and evocative covered

Walk 28 describes another, albeit short, stretch of the Strada Regia, between Brunate and Torno.

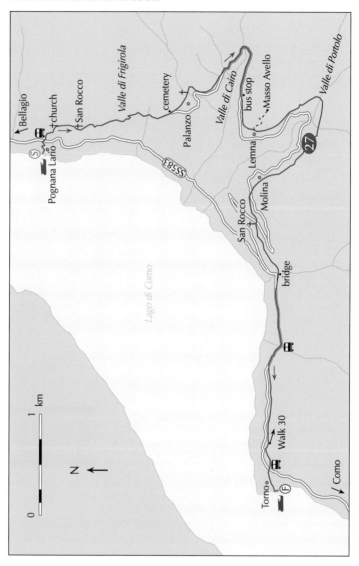

passageways. As the **church** tower comes into sight up ahead, branch R up to the building's entrance, which doubles as a superb viewing platform over the lake. Continue up past Via Crucis shrines to tarmac and a 'Strada Regia' sign. Still on Via Canzaga, keep uphill (S) past the last houses on a paved way bordered by stone walls. Past a water trough, it's not far to the sweeping outlook at **Chiesa di San Rocco**, a medieval church built on the site of a pagan temple.

Walk past the front and continue in the same direction on the clear wide track with occasional red/white paint-splash markers steadily uphill into woodland, where cascading streams are crossed on bridges in Valle di Frigirola. You emerge at the cemetery and car park at **Palanzo** (569m, 1hr). After the bus stop turn L up Via Pisciola past a bar to Piazza Sant'Ambrogio and the church in grey stone. To the right of the church steps take the old covered passageway Via Molino, which predictably (the name means 'mill'), leads across streams past an abandoned mill. Soon after keep R at a fork on a path with an iron railing, and gradually descend to join the road L, keeping an eye out for passing cars. Stick with the tarmac as it curves over the Valle di Cairo to a bus stop where you fork L. A quiet road takes you past another cemetery to the scenic piazza and Chiesa di San Giorgio at **Lemna** (569m, 40min).

*Lunch at Lemna*

147

*Crossing the stream
after Lemna*

Close at hand is a café-trattoria and an optional detour to a small tombstone from the 6th century, sculpted in an erratic boulder, as follows.

### Detour to Masso Avello at Bicogno (20min return)
At the trattoria turn L uphill on the stepped way out of the houses to where the ancient tomb stands on the edge of a field, with a lovely view over the village of Molina. Return to the trattoria to resume the Strada Regia.

From the trattoria turn R, then immediately L on Via Piana. At the ensuing fork keep R under a covered passageway, then next L under an archway where the tiny traditional houses are built on bare rock. At the next junction it's L to a picturesque fountain with a green spout. Here go R on Via Cappelletta past a villa and through vegetable gardens to a chapel with a circular bench. Keep R on a grassy path with an iron handrail for gentle ups and downs through woodland to a stony stream crossing in Valle di Portolo. Then it's NW up to a clearing where you can look back to Lemna and San Giorgio.

The route descends through the next village by way of an 1860 stone wash trough, before taking a tunnel-like passage below a building and into Piazza Sant'Antonio with the eponymous church at **Molina** (453m, 50min). ▸ Turn L on Via XX Settembre down to cross the road, continuing on a paved way in descent past houses through woodland to cut across the road once more, to the chapel of **San Rocco**.

Branch L here (Strada Regia sign), keeping down past a concrete wall to an old way, with stone walls. Soon an elegant **bridge** leads over a ravine and around to a gap in the trees with brilliant lake views. The busy main road is soon joined L, but only for a 5min stretch due W. After a bus stop and car park the lovely old path branches L, high over the tarmac. Further on are houses and tall stone walls around well-kept gardens and villas.

At the signed junction with the route from Piazzaga (see Walk 30) go diagonally R (Strada Regia sign) along the alley Via al Pozzo, continuing under covered passageways. It becomes stepped and finally curves R as Via Tridi, inexorably downhill past a playground to the main road and bus stop of **Torno** (239m, 50min). For the '*imbarcadero*' (ferry wharf, 10min) cross straight over and down to the divine lakeside and café.

The eatery Hostaria Antica specialises in tripe, though other 'easier' dishes are served and there's an adjoining grocery shop.

# WALK 28
*Brunate to Torno Path*

| | |
|---|---|
| **Start** | Brunate funicular station |
| **Finish** | Torno ferry wharf |
| **Distance** | 12.5km (7.7 miles) |
| **Ascent/Descent** | 250m/725m |
| **Difficulty** | Grade 2 |
| **Walking time** | 3hr 30min (+ 1hr extra side trips) |
| **Access** | The funicular cableway station at Como is located at the far eastern end of the waterfront, not far from the bus terminal and Trenord railway station. To return to Como, catch a ferry or bus from Torno. |

An immensely rewarding outing on the western side of the Lario peninsula, with a multitude of treats. The exciting funicular ride to Brunate (see Lago di Como Introduction) is immediately followed by a walk through woodland home to roe deer, through delightful mountain hamlets with splendid lake views and geological highlights: intriguing glacial erratics transported from Valtellina 60km to the north by the frozen rivers, abandoned like stranded whales when the ice masses retreated. Historical interest derives from the short stretch of Strada Regia, the 'royal road' followed here (see Walk 27). The walk concludes with a well-deserved drink at the lakeside and a leisurely ferry ride back to Como. What more could anyone ask of a day out?

The route can be shortened by taking a direct descent to Torno instead of following the Piazzaga loop. Take supplies for a panoramic picnic as no cafés are encountered; Montepiatto has a trattoria although it opens only on weekends (tel 031 419446).

Another beautiful section of the Strada Regia, between Pognana Lario and Torno, is described in Walk 27.

◄ On arrival at the funicular station at **Brunate** (715m) get your breath back and admire the city of Como at your feet, the ancient moraine ridges and even Monte Rosa, then take the steps in descent either side of the station to the road and viewpoint immediately over the cables. As per the Strada Regia sign, turn R past an old Campari fountain, then L down Via Nidrino with lovely Art Deco villas and Swiss-style chalets. You skirt the R edge of a playing field (**Centro Sportivo**) to a sign pointing you R onto a path flanking houses and N into woodland. Narrow at times and with minor ups and downs and stretches of

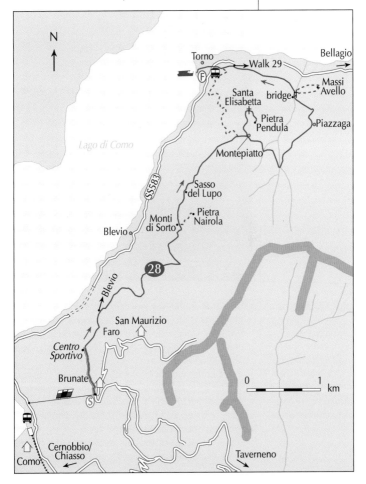

*View from the top of the funicular at Brunate*

After leaving Brunate the route through woodland is subject to minor landslips that tear away small sections of path. Maintenance is usually prompt, but take a little extra care.

cable handrail, the way proceeds through damp woodland with ferns and cyclamen flowers and ongoing water views. After a fork, where a path from Blevio joins up, the path widens and improves, shifting NE but curving in and out of side valleys past minor waterfalls. ◄

At a bridge (and another path from Blevio) continue following signs for Montepiatto on to the path junction at **Monti di Sorto** (520m, 1hr 15min), complete with a chapel, fountain and benches. There are lovely views across west to Cernobbio and the villas.

The extension to the first erratic boulder, Pietra Nairola, begins here:

**Pietra Nairola side trip (40min return)**
**Note** The steep path can be slippery. Turn R up the narrow zigzagging path to the perch of **Pietra Nairola** (620m). Appearing to totter on the slope, the 300-ton granite boulder was deposited here by a glacier which transported it from Val Masino, which branches off Valtellina at the top of Lago di Como. Return the same way to Monti di Sorto, taking extra care on the steep sections.

*The Pietra Nairola*

The clear path continues past houses due N through the wood. Not far along is the absolutely gigantic glacier erratic, 4000-ton Sasso del Lupo, apparently in the process of sliding down the hillside. ▸

The 'wolf's rock' is so called as the hollow at its base was believed to have been the den of a dreaded wolf that ensnared disobedient children!

Soon, at a cluster of houses, keep R at a fork, in imperceptible ascent NE past huts old and abandoned. This leads on to join the paved mule track that ascends from the lakeside, a feasible exit route if needed, as follows.

**Exit to Torno (40min)**
Turn L for the steady 400m descent down to the main road, then the lakeside and ferry wharf at **Torno** (205m).

Turn R uphill to the nearby houses of **Montepiatto** (614m, 45min), sadly all but uninhabited apart from during holiday periods. At a tap make sure you fork L for the 'Chiesa' (church). In and out of the stone buildings you walk N across to the wonderful terrace of the **Chiesa di Santa Elisabetta** (45min). Shaded picnic tables welcome walkers to drink in the fantastic view over this narrow stretch of Lago di Como, and to Monte San Primo (northeast), the zenith of the Triangolo Lariano.

From the church, a sign points SE to another curious glacial boulder dubbed **Pietra Pendula**. A mere 60 tons, this too came from Val Masino. Granite in composition, it stands on an eroded limestone stalk, resembling a mushroom. Retrace your steps via the church and back to the main mule track through Montepiatto (30min).

*Montepiatto is set in dense woodland*

Turn L and on to the sign for Piazzaga where you go R on a paved way past Trattoria Crotto, leaving the houses behind. At a junction with a crucifix continue on the lane SE at first and mostly level. About 1.5km on, as it begins climbing, leave it for a signed path that forks off L in gentle descent through trees to a shrine in the modest settlement of **Piazzaga** (574m). Branch L (NW) down the surprisingly steep lane that becomes a long sequence of steps. These are masterfully fashioned from strips of non-slip granite sliced off an erratic boulder (necessity is the mother of invention!). Past pylons and into the woodland, it curves this way and that to a turn-off. This is an optional loop via more erratics.

### Negrenza and Massi Avelli loop (20min)
Follow the narrow path R to visit the fascinating pre-Roman tombs scooped out of erratic boulders and the abandoned hamlet of Negrenza (430m). Keep on L (W) and out to rejoin the main route at the bridge and ravine.

The way descends to a bridge (400m) over a ravine, with an adjoining chapel where the Massi Avelli loop joins back up.

Cross the bridge and descend WNW on the old mule track, edged with a low stone wall, as it curves around the mountain and through an old gateway. Pasture, orchards and well-tended vegetable gardens line the way before the first houses of Torno are reached. At the signed junction go diagonally L (Strada Regia) along the alley Via al Pozzo, continuing under a covered passageways. It becomes stepped, and finally curves R as Via Tridi, inexorably downhill past a playground to the main road and bus stop of **Torno** (239m, 1hr). For the '*imbarcadero*' (ferry wharf, 10min) cross straight over and down to the divine lakeside complete with a café, a short stroll away.

*The Strada Regia in Torno*

*The walk concludes at the pretty lakeside of Torno*

# SENTIERO DEL VIANDANTE TREK

*The approach to Corenno Plinio (Stage 5)*

# SENTIERO DEL VIANDANTE TREK

*The Wayfarer's Path from Lecco to Colico*

| | |
|---|---|
| **Start** | Lecco railway station |
| **Finish** | Colico railway station |
| **Distance** | 54.3km (33.7 miles) |
| **Ascent/Descent** | 2170m/2170m |
| **Difficulty** | Grade 2 (short 2–3 sections in Stage 3) |
| **Walking time** | 19hr 10min – 5 days |
| **Access** | Trains from Milano Centrale run to Lecco and all stations to Colico |

The Sentiero del Viandante (abbreviated as SdV) is a rewarding five-day route northwards along the eastern edge of Lago di Como. The 'Wayfarer's Path' follows historical tracks linking Lombardy with alpine valleys and Switzerland trodden by traders and herders.

Far from being a lakeside stroll, it alternates climbs to age-old mountainside hamlets with panoramic traverses and descends into waterfront villages clustered around minuscule harbours. Sheer-sided mountains tower overhead, starting with the renowned Grigne.

The mini trek is well signposted and is not especially difficult, following wide, paved tracks and narrower mountain paths. Drinking water can be replenished in most villages thanks to fountains and taps, whereas lunch supplies are best purchased before setting out each day.

All the stage ends offer accommodation and excellent evening meals, not to mention romantic lakeside promenades and several pebbly beaches for a dip. Moreover, thanks to the good train services as well as occasional ferries, the walk can be done in single day stages if you prefer to return to the same base each night.

**Note:** The SdV has recently been extended northwards via Morbegno in Valtellina and up Val Masino to San Martino in Val di Mello, but this is not covered here.

## STAGE 1
*Lecco to Abbadia Lariana*

| | |
|---|---|
| **Start** | Lecco railway station |
| **Finish** | Abbadia Lariana railway station |
| **Distance** | 7.7km (4.8 miles) |
| **Ascent/Descent** | 150m/150m |
| **Difficulty** | Grade 2 |
| **Walking time** | 2hr 40min |

After a stroll along the attractive lakeside at Lecco in the company of swans, clear paths lead through shady woodland, cutting across steep mountainsides and dodging rockfall barriers.

**Note:** Although worthwhile, be aware that this stage is not always peaceful due to the proximity of sections of busy highway. You can always catch a train or ferry to Abbadia Lariana and start there with Stage 2 if you prefer.

*The lakefront at Lecco looks towards the mountainous north*

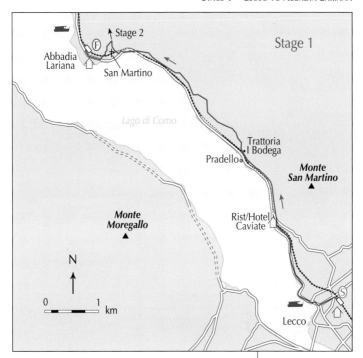

Leave Lecco railway station (216m) via the west exit (*lato ovest*) and take the street straight ahead. It immediately curves R, passing the old town walls, to where an official Sentiero del Viandante sign points L down narrow pedestrian Via G Bovara.

Continue past shops to the lake. There, go R along the shady walkway past the ferry landing stage and cafés, enjoying excellent views. Where the promenade ends at a petrol station, the SdV parts ways with a cycle track (which continues along the lakefront) and crosses the road, continuing to **Ristorante/Hotel Caviate** (tel 0341 367583 www.caviate.it). Here, go R on narrow Via dell'Abbadia and over the railway line to the start of the actual path (n.505), which is well signposted.

*The signed route begins its climb away from the road*

Steps climb into woodland to follow a raised embankment, where massive steel netting provides protection from rockfalls from Monte San Martino. Further along, a short stretch of tarmac leads above Pradello to well-reputed café-restaurant **Trattoria I Bodega** (1hr 20min) which is handy for lunch – if you don't mind the proximity of the road flyover and trains.

Now the clear, if narrow, path heads along the base of a mountain, where multiple climbing routes are marked. It later descends around more hefty barriers before embarking on several testing ups and downs. After a large water conduit, it finally veers L over the railway and road, to where stairs lead down towards the lakeside.

At their foot, keep R but not far along, don't miss the fork R away from the waterfront. At the church of **San Martino** an old way leads up past houses. At a flight of steps ignore the SdV (unless you're proceeding directly with Stage 2) and turn L on Via Onedo. Down at the main road go R for the nearby railway station and the Park Hotel (tel 0341 730030 www.hotelparkcomolago. com) of **Abbadia Lariana** (214m, 1hr 20min). For the ferry wharf head L to the lakefront.

Do find time for the delightful lakefront promenade.

*The path below
Monte San Martino*

## STAGE 2

*Abbadia Lariana to Lierna*

| | |
|---|---|
| **Start** | Abbadia Lariana railway station |
| **Finish** | Lierna railway station |
| **Distance** | 10.8km (6.7 miles) |
| **Ascent/Descent** | 300m/300m |
| **Difficulty** | Grade 2 |
| **Walking time** | 3hr 15min |

An excellent varied stage with long sections of old cobbled ways through fields and wood, touching on churches and quiet villages. Needless to say, lovely lake and mountain views are a constant! Today the route climbs high, well above Mandello del Lario, which is home to the world-famous Guzzi motorbikes. A renowned eatery and B&B are encountered an hour into the walk, should you need them.

*Paths through fields lead to mountainside villages*

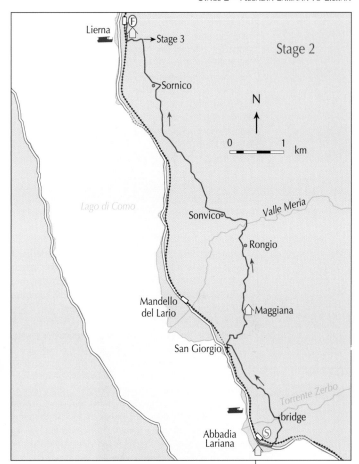

From the railway station at Abbadia Lariana (214m) follow the main road E (in the direction of Lecco) to where Via Onedo forks L uphill. Curving R, it reaches a small flight of steps and an SdV sign. Turn L, soon on a narrow cobbled way running between houses and fields: a lovely stretch.

Ignore turn-offs and keep on to cross a **bridge** over Torrente Zerbo, the river responsible for creating Abbadia's alluvial fan. Not long after a showy shrine is a handy café/shop (Gastronomia Il Viandante) where they rustle up tasty panini for walkers. You soon veer L under the highway, then immediately sharp R on a quiet, shady lane. Cypresses stand tall around the Romanesque church of San Giorgio. (If you strike lucky and it's open, pop in to admire the frescoes.) An abrupt R turn leads uphill to where you cross the highway. Then keep L on the lane but take care not to miss the fork R for a quiet path through fields. Up at the peaceful village of **Maggiana** (339m, 1hr) are accommodation (B&B Alla Torre del Barbarossa tel 0341 733715 or 338 6447079 www.allatorredelbarbarossa.it) and restaurant Osteria Sali e Tabacchi.

Signs point you past the medieval tower Torre di Barbarossa, where Holy Roman Emperor Frederick I stayed in far-off 1158. More ascent follows, well below the feet of the soaring Grigne peaks, and fields give way to chestnut trees as the shady way resumes N. You traverse **Rongio** (394m), where there is a shop and café, before a road plunges towards the Al Verde restaurant. A tad before it, the SdV branches R then soon L as a path into lovely **Valle Meria**, with a cascading stream and a fascinating natural rock bridge. Naturally, what goes down must go up; you puff up to a road where it's L into **Sonvico** (377m) for a view over Olcio.

Descent leads through orchards and olive groves to walls adorned with the writings of a local poet and past a shrine. Then, you follow a concreted lane flanking the busy highway, but not for long. After a water trough you enter tiny **Sornico** hamlet, exiting via an arch under a house. Down the road, follow signs on the old way Via Chignola. Further along, this joins a road down to a T-junction – go R but very soon you need to fork L for Lierna (orange arrows on the ground) on a stepped way. Via Genico descends to the post office near the train line – go R along Via Parodi to the station of **Lierna** (212m).

*You leave Sornico via an archway under a house*

On the other side of the railway, accommodation includes B&B Patrizia (tel 348 9349188 www.bbpatrizia. com) and B&B Le Fate del Lago (tel 348 2896467 http:// fatedellago.it) in the old part of the village. The ferry wharf is a short distance downhill.

While here, do find time for the attractive waterfront promenade leading to the fascinating old Castello district and the modest beach.

# STAGE 3

*Lierna to Varenna*

| | |
|---|---|
| **Start** | Lierna railway station |
| **Finish** | Varenna railway station |
| **Distance** | 10.3km (6.4 miles) |
| **Ascent/Descent** | 780m/780m |
| **Difficulty** | Grade 2–3 |
| **Walking time** | 4hr 15min |

This stage spells drawn-out ascent, every single metre of which is amply rewarded by stunning views from a string of lookouts that double as memorable picnic spots. Be aware that the final descent can be challenging on the knees.

**Note:** A short distance from the stage start, the SdV splits into two: the *variante alta* (high variant) and *variante bassa* (low variant). Although the latter is marginally shorter and entails less ascent, it includes a stretch alongside the highway and is nowhere near as scenic. The route described here is the *variante alta*, which is more popular and preferable.

*It's a long climb after Genico*

From Lierna railway station (212m) take Via Parodi R (S) as far as the post office and turn uphill on Via Genico. Where a flight of steps reaches a road, keep straight ahead and then go around a corner L to the SdV fork: go R on the *variante alta* (aka n.71) past a B&B to the hamlet of **Genico** (320m), complete with fountain and sun dial.

Soon you dip below the highway and onto a surprisingly steep, concreted lane that quickly becomes a sunken path in shady woodland. Beneath sheer cliffs,

*The lookout at Alpe Mezzedo*

tall rock steps aid the ascent N – 'relentless' comes to mind. A side stream precedes the huge cross **Croce del Brentalone** (650m), where marvellous views can be admired from picnic tables. Path n.71 continues to the pasture clearings of **Alpe Mezzedo** (871m), where there is a fountain and a detour to another lookout. Still in shady woodland the way climbs to a new lane, where you turn L to the minuscule chapel of **San Pietro** (992m, 2hr). This comes complete with a rest area and a magnificent outlook taking in Bellagio, the lake branch towards Como and mountains galore.

Follow the lane through beech woodland via a pond in gentle descent to a road and the scattered houses of **Ortanella** (958m). Here, continue N on the road, which soon becomes a rough lane that rounds Monte Fopp, high over a side valley containing the village of Esino Lario. A marked path finally branches R for the start of the drawn-out plunging descent. It's mostly in beautiful wood land that provides welcome shade, while openings spell heart-stopping views to the lake. The way follows a narrowing crest where chestnut trees abound; loose stones are rife underfoot – watch your step. The occassional landmarks include a ruined hut then the cross **Croce del Fopp** (577m).

A sunken path leads past abandoned huts on the last leg to the peaceful village of **Vezio** (350m, 2hr). Here, you can rest, enjoy a refreshing drink at the café-restaurant, stay overnight at Il Portichetto (tel 327 3432093 www.hotelilportichetto.it), visit the modest Castello (www.castellodivezio.it) or take the well-kept paved way downhill. This concludes on the road near **Olivedo**: go R for the railway station and ferry wharf but turn L for nearby **Varenna** (217m, 15min).

A charming laidback village, with its near-vertical stepped alleys, Varenna is well geared to tourists, with attractive lakeside eateries, a *passeggiata lungolago* (lakeside promenade) and accommodation such as Albergo Milano (tel 0341 830298 www.albergomilanovarenna.com). Find time to visit the terraced gardens of Villa Cipressi, incredibly squeezed in between the sheer mountain flanks, road and lake.

*Evening light over Lago di Como from Varenna*

# STAGE 4

*Varenna to Dervio*

| | |
|---|---|
| **Start** | Varenna railway station |
| **Finish** | Dervio railway station |
| **Distance** | 12.5km (7.8 miles) |
| **Ascent/Descent** | 530m/530m |
| **Difficulty** | Grade 2 |
| **Walking time** | 4hr 45min |

A ramble through woodland and charming old hamlets best describes this stage. Along the way, attentive walkers will notice manmade cavities at the base of old stone walls, where water draining off the mountainsides accumulates – this was used for livestock and irrigation.

About halfway today is Bellano with a dramatic *orrido*/ravine that is worth taking time out to visit.the highway and is nowhere as near as scenic. The route described here is the *variante alta*, more popular and preferable.

From Varenna railway station (220m) walk downhill to the main road and go L to where cobbled pedestrian Via alla Croce branches L. (If starting from the ferry wharf, go up the stepped way Via alla Riva to the R of Hotel Olivedo, where it crosses the main road and continues as Via della Croce). A short way up you're pointed sharp L, winding past houses and into woodland. Ignore turnoffs and continue to **Vezio** (350m, 30min) and a path junction. The village offers a café-restaurant, accommodation at Il Portichetto (tel 327 3432093 www.hotelilportichetto. it) and a modest castle www.castellodivezio.it.

Turn L (E) at the junction, down a steepish paved path, thick with wild mint bushes, to an old bridge spanning Torrente Esino. Up on the other side at a road you do a quick dogleg R then L past a small factory to where the stepped SdV resumes uphill. This takes you to the lovely

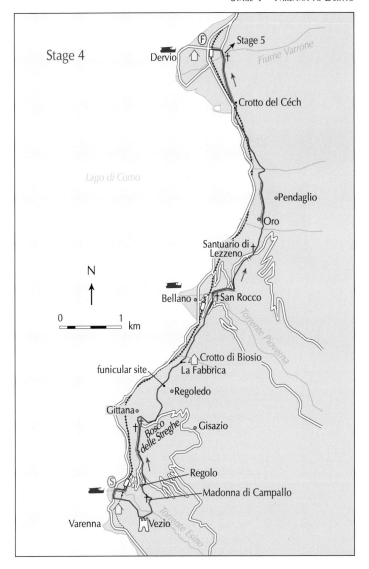

*The old bridge spanning Torrente Esino*

Baroque chapel of **Madonna di Campallo** with its cypress trees, graceful archway and frescoed interior. With lovely lake views, the path proceeds through olive groves on its way to the village of **Regolo** (320m), home to Piazza Bassa and a church.

Now ignore the SdV sign R for Perledo (unless you need a café, as this takes a longer road loop), and veer L on Via degli Orti, uphill, past a car park to cross a road, and continue on a shady way between high stone walls. At a fork with a shrine keep L (not uphill for Bosco delle Streghe) – this is the official SdV once more. At a minor road follow the tarmac in ascent through an old quarry and past a small council tip. At a nearby **chapel** on a corner the path resumes L. Dropping through woodland, this touches on a church then meets a road where you go R. Only metres along, take the shady way off L, climbing past a cemetery and onto a wide level stretch. Keep straight ahead as per SdV signs, ignoring turn-offs to the hamlets of Gittana and Gisazio.

Not long after a timber bridge you cross a man-made ravine that once featured a remarkable piece of engineering – a hydraulic-powered **funicular**. From 1903 until the 1950s it transported passengers up to Regoledo, where a spa resort had begun operations in 1851, hosting guests the like of Italian conductor Arturo Toscanini no less!

The peaceful way proceeds NE between drystone walls and looks down to Bellano and the upper spread of the lake. The next landmark is **La Fabbrica**, an elegant, traditional house dating back 300 years and long used as an inn for wayfarers. Here, go L (or R for a 5min detour to eatery/accommodation **Crotto di Biosio** tel 0341 821361

*Bellano can be seen through the trees*

www.biosio.it) for the start of the long descent. Not far
down are picnic tables in case you should feel the need
for a rest.

A bridge is crossed and you're high above houses
and the railway station. An extensive block of long-
abandoned factories stretches out towards the waterfront.
Cross a road and go R for 150 metres to where the paved
way resumes to Torrente Pioverna, which flows through
an awesome *orrido* (ravine) many dizzy metres under-
neath. Formed 15 million years ago by the torrential
melting waters of the Adda glacier, it has been fitted out
with suspended walkways and is well worth a visit for a
modest fee.

Over a bridge stands the white **Chiesa di San Rocco**
(240m, 1hr 45min) at **Bellano**.

(To exit the walk here, turn L down the stepped way
past the gated entrance to the *orrido*. At the bottom of
the steps, at a church, keep L past an old cotton mill to
the main road, and L again across the river. Take the first
main street L for the railway station (206m, 15min). To
reach the *imbarcadero* (ferry wharf), go R along the main
road through to the lakeside.)

Turn R on Via per Ombriaco, flanking the cemetery
wall. The lane climbs long and steadily, under roads and
past blocks of flats. It finally reaches a signed junction at
a wash trough and forks L along a paved alley through a
residential zone. Proceeding NNE, it crosses the road
twice en route to the huge, cream-coloured 18th-century
**Santuario di Lezzeno** (370m, 1hr) and a quiet hamlet
with a shady picnic area. Detour L to the marvellous lake
viewpoint; Monte Grona and the Bregagnino stand out
on the western shore directly opposite.

From the front of the church go R then L, then turn
R along a signed alley through to the road. SdV signs
then guide you through a charming cluster of old houses
before touching on the road (close to a bus stop) with a
clear view to the Dervio peninsula. A gentle uphill path is
followed, and another road crossed, then a lovely lengthy
cobbled section ensues, threading its way past tiny farms
and fields where fig, walnut and cherry trees abound.

*Steep ramps of steps down to Bellano*

A downhill leg runs parallel to the road before traversing a ravine alive with crashing cascades and passing a ruined mill building (Molino di Oro).

Not far on, at a house, ignore the fork for Pendaglio and go downhill to the road towards the village of **Oro** (279m). Turn R along the asphalt, keeping R at a fork, then go steeply uphill past rural properties to a car park. Here, the SdV proceeds straight ahead as a path.

With more uphill past old houses, a lovely well-signed section, cobbled in parts, heads N through woodland and fields with views towards Dervio and its promontory. Gentle descent leads through chestnut trees and across a watercourse. A short climb leads past rock flanks overlooking the railway line and warehouses. Finally, steps lead down to the road and a renowned local restaurant (**Crotto del Céch** tel 0341 804227). Walk R along Via Duca d'Aosta for 800 metres. You pass a beautiful, tiny Romanesque church then cross the bridge spanning the Fiume Varrone, which was responsible for forming the peninsula occupied by **Dervio** (238m, 1hr 15min).

(For the ferry wharf, take the third street L – Via Martiri della Liberazione – over the railway line and continue towards the waterfront. For the railway station, take the fourth street on the L – Via XX Settembre.)

Accommodation includes La Casa sul Sasso (tel 347 3191372 www.bbcstone.com).

# STAGE 5
*Dervio to Colico*

| | |
|---|---|
| **Start** | Dervio railway station |
| **Finish** | Colico railway station |
| **Distance** | 13km (8 miles) |
| **Ascent/descent** | 440m/440m |
| **Difficulty** | Grade 2 |
| **Walking time** | 4hr 15min |

This excellent concluding stage drops in on charming lakeside Corenno Plinio – which begs to be explored. The SdV then embarks on marvellous paved lanes and paths that surmount a final ridge separating you from the northern end of the lake and its spectacular crown of Alps. Awesome views are constant companions today.

From the railway station at Dervio, walk through to the main road and take Via al Castello. It soon joins up with the SdV (aka Via Giglio, which turns off the main road just after the river bridge in Stage 4).

Once you reach a side road, an old stepped way breaks off R for a puff-inducing climb to **Castello** (274m). You circle the old tower before following tarmac past a wash house and under a raised road. Down at a junction follow the signed way in descent through woodland to join a road (near Hotel Oasi del Viandante). Turn R to reach a crossroads at a **road tunnel** then L on quiet Via del Monastero. Some 600 metres on, the tarmac gives way to the delightful original paved path with stone steps that take you to the roadside and Piazza Garibaldi at **Corenno Plinio** (231m, 40min).

This charming village boasting hundreds of steps, a café-restaurant, castle and a frescoed church named after St Thomas of Canterbury, is well worth time out. Don't miss the viewpoint below the castle.

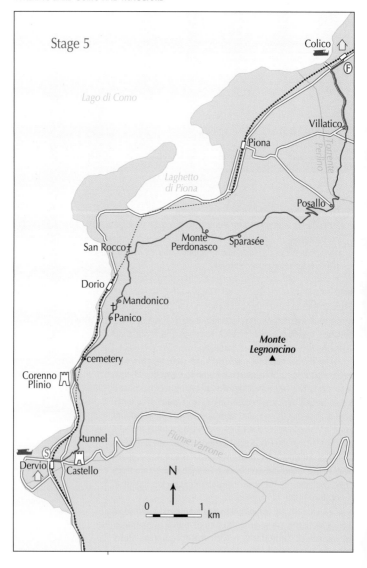

Stage 5

Colico

*Lago di Como*

Villatico

Piona

*Torrente Perlino*

*Laghetto di Piona*

Posallo

Monte
Perdonasco

Sparasée

San Rocco

Dorio

Mandonico

Panico

*Monte Legnoncino*

cemetery

Corenno
Plinio

*Fiume Varrone*

tunnel

Dervio

Castello

N

0    1    km

Walk N along the main road for a matter of metres then branch R on Via Maronasso, a grassy lane leading to the cemetery. A gentle climb past buildings is followed by a short stretch of tarmac past the houses of **Panico.** At a car park the old way, lined with stone walls, resumes, climbing to the church of San Giorgio (and a link with Dorio and the railway if needed). Not far up is the ghost village of **Mandonico** (302m), in a time warp. People once chose to live here, well above the lake shore, as it guaranteed protection from the passage of marauding armies.

Climbing steadily through tree heather and cistus bushes, the superb way reaches the awesome lookout at the chapel of **San Rocco** (487m, 1hr 10min) whete there are picnic tables and a tap. The chapel was erected in 1858 by the people of Dorio after an outbreak of cholera.

*The lakefront at Corenno Plinio*

The underlying rock here has smoothed surfaces, a clear sign of glacial moulding.

Once a broad saddle has been traversed in chestnut woodland, vast views of the head of Lago di Como open up, with broad Valtellina and the Adda river, as well as the Laghetto di Piona, an inlet. You continue NE with ups and downs, through the long-abandoned hamlet of Rossecco with its flights of steps cut into the rock. Nearby are the summer holiday houses of **Monte Perdonasco** (616m) then continue to **Sparasée** and a gushing stream and fountain. A car park spells the end of the old way and the start of a quiet road, concreted at first. A few short cuts beckon on the descent to **Posallo** (433m, 1hr 40min) and a family run café-*trattoria*.

*From San Rocco walkers are rewarded with vast views down the lake*

Not far down the road the SdV forks R up and over a stream. After the crossing turn sharp L, leaving the SdV signage (it has been extended into Valtellina), for a rough lane through fields heading N. You join a road continuing downhill to the village of **Villatico** – keep R then L, as per the Sentiero dei Torrenti route. Past a church go straight ahead to the main road at **Colico** (218m). Continue under the railway line for the lakefront, and the chance of a dip, and cafés, otherwise turn R for the railway station (45min).

Accommodation includes Hotel Risi (tel 0341 933089 www.hotelrisi.com).

*Beautiful views are enjoyed over the Piona inlet and the northern reaches of Lago di Como*

# APPENDIX A
*Route summary table*

| Walk no/Walk title | | Time | Distance | Ascent/ Descent | Grade | Page |
|---|---|---|---|---|---|---|
| 1 | Stresa to Belgirate | 2hr 40min | 9km (5.6 miles) | 300m/270m | 1–2 | 29 |
| 2 | From the Mottarone to Baveno | 3hr 50min | 15km (9.3 miles) | 0m/1300m | 2+ | 33 |
| 3 | Monte Orfano and Lago di Mergozzo | 4hr | 13km (8 miles) | 600m/600m | 2–3 | 38 |
| 4 | Cavandone on Monterosso | 2hr 30min | 8.5km (5.3 miles) | 265m/265m | 1–2 | 43 |
| 5 | Ghiffa Sanctuary Loop | 3hr | 10.5km (6.5 miles) | 565m/565m | 1–2 | 47 |
| 6 | Villages above Cannero | 4hr | 16.5km (10.3 miles) | 800m/800m | 2 | 51 |
| 7 | The Cannero– Cannobio Traverse | 2hr 20min | 8.5km (5.3 miles) | 420m/420m | 1–2 | 55 |
| 8 | Monte Carza | 5hr | 17km (10.6 miles) | 900m/900m | 2–3 | 59 |
| 9 | Val Cannobina | 5hr | 20km (12.4 miles) | 700m/1150m | 2 | 63 |
| 10 | Cannobio–San Bartolomeo in Montibus Circuit | 3hr 40min | 12km (7.5 miles) | 450m/450m | 2 | 69 |
| 11 | Monteviasco | 4hr | 15.6km (9.7 miles) | 800m/800m | 1–2 | 73 |
| 12 | Sasso del Ferro | 2hr 30min | 8.5km (5.3 miles) | 110m/850m | 2 | 78 |
| 13 | Moltrasio to Laglio | 1hr 45min | 5.2km (3.2 miles) | 150m/150m | 1–2 | 90 |
| 14 | Pigra to Colonno | 2hr | 5.8km (3.6 miles) | 50m/660m | 2 | 93 |
| 15 | Colonno to Cadenabbia on the Greenway | 3hr 15min | 10.5km (6.5 miles) | 100m/100m | 1 | 96 |

| Walk no/Walk title | | Time | Distance | Ascent/Descent | Grade | Page |
|---|---|---|---|---|---|---|
| 16 | San Martino Circuit | 2hr 30min | 5.7km (3.5 miles) | 250m/250m | 2 | 101 |
| 17 | The Bocchetta di Nava Traverse | 3hr 15min | 9km (5.6 miles) | 500m/685m | 2 | 104 |
| 18 | Crocetta | 1hr | 3.5km (2.2 miles) | 110m/110m | 1 | 108 |
| 19 | Val Sanagra | 5hr 20min | 14km (8.7 miles) | 550m/550m | 2 | 111 |
| 20 | Rifugio Menaggio and Monte Grona | 4hr 40min | 9km (5.6 miles) | 950m/950m | 2+ | 116 |
| 21 | San Domenico and the Santuario di Breglia | 1hr 15min | 3km (1.8 miles) | 60m/60m | 1 | 121 |
| 22 | Gravedona to Domaso | 1hr 30min | 4km (2.5 miles) | 200m/200m | 1–2 | 123 |
| 23 | Domaso to Gera Lario | 2hr 20min | 7.5km (4.6 miles) | 280m/280m | 2 | 127 |
| 24 | Around Bellagio | 2hr | 6km (3.7 miles) | 85m/85m | 1 | 133 |
| 25 | Belvedere del Monte Nuvolone | 4hr 15min | 14km (8.7 miles) | 1130m/240m | 2 | 137 |
| 26 | Monte San Primo | 3hr 20min | 7.5km (4.6 miles) | 580m/580m | 2+ | 141 |
| 27 | The Strada Regia from Pognana Lario to Torno | 3hr 30min | 10.5km (6.5 miles) | 360m/360m | 1–2 | 145 |
| 28 | Brunate to Torno Path | 3hr 30min | 12.5km (7.7 miles) | 250m/725m | 2 | 150 |
| Sentiero del Viandante Trek | | 19hr 10min (5 days) | 54.3km (33.7 miles) | 2170m/2170m | 2 | 156 |

# APPENDIX B

*Glossary of Italian–English terms*

| Italian | English |
| --- | --- |
| *acqua (non) potabile* | (un)drinkable water |
| *affittacamere* | B&B |
| *aiuto!* | help! |
| *albergo* | hotel |
| *alimentari* | grocery shop |
| *aperto/chiuso* | open/closed |
| *aria di sosta* | picnic area |
| *attracco, imbarcadero, pontile, scalo* | ferry pier, wharf, landing stage |
| *autostazione* | bus station |
| *baita* | mountain hut, often a rustic restaurant |
| *battello* | passenger ferry |
| *bivio* | junction |
| *bocca, bocchetta* | saddle, pass (lit. mouth, little mouth) |
| *bosco* | wood |
| *caduta massi/sassi* | rockfalls |
| *calchera* | lime kiln |
| *cappella* | shrine, chapel |
| *carta escursionistica* | walking map |
| *castello* | castle |
| *centro storico* | historic town centre |
| *chiesa* | church |
| *cima* | peak |

| Italian | English |
| --- | --- |
| *cimitero* | cemetery |
| *comune, municipio* | town hall |
| *corriere, autobus* | bus |
| *costone, cresta, crinale, dorsale* | crest, ridge |
| *croce* | cross |
| *crotto* | originally a cave, now a rustic restaurant |
| *destra/sinistra* | right/left |
| *deviazione* | detour |
| *difficile/facile* | difficult/easy |
| *eremo* | hermitage |
| *faro* | lighthouse |
| *fermata dell'autobus* | bus stop |
| *fiume* | river |
| *foce* | estuary |
| *forno* | oven, furnace |
| *frana* | landslide |
| *funicolare* | funicular lift |
| *funivia* | cable car |
| *galleria* | tunnel |
| *gradinata* | flight of steps |
| *guado* | stream or river ford |
| *imbarcadero* | ferry wharf |
| *incisione rupestre* | rock engraving |
| *inferiore/superiore* | lower/upper |

| Italian | English |
|---------|---------|
| *isola* | island |
| *lago* | lake |
| *lungolago* | lakefront promenade |
| *maneggio* | horse riding |
| *molino, mulino* | mill |
| *montagna, monte, monti* | mountain or high-altitude pasture |
| *mulattiera* | old mule track |
| *orario* | timetable |
| *orrido* | ravine |
| *panificio* | bakery |
| *passeggiata pedonale* | pedestrian promenade |
| *pasticceria* | cake shop |
| *pedoni* | pedestrians |
| *pericolo!* | danger! |
| *piazza* | village or town square |
| *pizzo, vetta* | peak |
| *ponte* | bridge |
| *previsioni del tempo* | weather forecast |
| *pronto soccorso* | first aid/emergency ward |
| *rifugio* | mountain hut |

| Italian | English |
|---------|---------|
| *rio, torrente* | mountain stream |
| *ristoro* | refreshments, café |
| *scalinata* | flight of steps |
| *scorciatoia* | shortcut |
| *seggiovia* | chair lift |
| *sentiero* | path |
| *soccorso alpino* | mountain rescue |
| *sorgente* | spring (water) |
| *sottopassaggio* | underpass |
| *spiaggia* | beach |
| *stazione ferroviaria* | railway station |
| *sterrata* | lane, unsurfaced road |
| *strada, via* | road |
| *supermercato* | supermarket |
| *teleferica* | goods cableway |
| *torre* | tower |
| *traghetto* | car ferry |
| *trattoria* | rustic-style restaurant |
| *vecchio, vecchia* | old |

*Approaching San Martino the path has a wonderful outlook on the lake (Walk 16)*

# NOTES